THE PARTI
REVENUE REVOLUTION

Transforming Ecosystems Into Profitable Efficient Growth Engines!

BY

CRAIG BOOTH

ABOUT CRAIG BOOTH

Thank you for purchasing the book, I hope you get value from the strategies and frameworks presented. Let me tell you a little about me, I am an author and thought leader in the field of channel sales and partner ecosystems. I have several decades of experience delivering revenue growth through innovative partnership strategies. I am the founder of Channel Force Incorporated which has become a trusted advisor to many leading companies looking to optimize their go-to-market approaches. As the author of the book "Channel Force" and the new release "The Partner-Powered Revenue Revolution," I love to delve deep into the intricacies of revenue creation, with a goal of offering practical insights and frameworks to transform the way businesses harness the power of their partner networks.

My 30 year career is marked by the ability to blend strategic thinking with actionable tactics, making complex concepts accessible and implementable. My expertise spans across various industries, providing me with a unique perspective on the challenges and opportunities within the channel sales landscape. Through my consulting practice, I strive to empower organizations to navigate the ever-evolving market dynamics and achieve sustainable growth.

Beyond my writing, I am a speaker and consultant, known for

his engaging presentations and hands-on workshops and inspiring professionals to rethink and revitalize their channel strategies. With "Channel Force" and "The Partner-Powered Revenue Revolution," the books pioneer a new approach to partner sales innovation, guiding businesses towards modern partnering models that produce efficient and profitable revenue growth.

TABLE OF CONTENTS

INTRODUCTION

"My biggest channel sales challenges are partner-led growth and articulating the value of my partner ecosystem to the *Board of Directors"*- Every CRO

In 2023, the tech sector experienced significant job losses, with more than 260,000 positions eliminated due to layoffs, affecting even high-ranking officials like Revenue Leaders and Partnership Leaders. Channel sales leadership, in particular, faced substantial impacts. Throughout the year, I helped numerous former vice presidents of channel sales in their job searches. The question arises: why were these skilled and highly talented partnership leaders without jobs? While the immediate response might point to the broader economic downturn, the issue runs deeper. As organizations increasingly prioritize Profitable Efficient Growth (PEG), revenue leaders who cannot clearly link their strategies to tangible outcomes find their value within the sales hierarchy diminished.

As artificial intelligence continues to expand and pose a potential threat to job security, demonstrating performance and efficiency has become increasingly critical. This challenge is particularly pronounced in partnership models, which inherently suffer from a lack of visibility and alignment between partner enablement and actual deal closure. The indirect nature of partnerships, combined with an opaque view into the partners' prospecting efforts, makes it exceedingly difficult to establish a direct connection between the partnership process and the final sales results (attribution).

The problem is traditional approaches to indirect sales lack a systematic approach to partner-sourced demand creation. Every partnership go-to-market model is based on "partner and pray" approaches that lack structured sales performance and predictable revenue outcomes. This chaotic approach leads to valuing partner-level metrics that are circumstantial evidence of partner activity explaining the "What," but never the "How," "When," or "Why" for outcomes. This lack of transparency and the inefficiency of opportunistic partnering models is devaluing the partnering function, putting jobs at risk.

Today's focus on sales efficiency and cost of sales has cast a spotlight on the channel. The ad hoc and opportunistic nature of conventional partnering models demands considerable resources for partner recruitment, enablement, and management, leading to a prolonged period before realizing value from new partnerships. Nonetheless, when executed effectively, a partnership model can vastly outperform strategies that rely solely on direct sales. The question then becomes how does an organization combine the extensive reach and rapid execution of partner sales with the transparency and oversight characteristic of direct sales models.

This is where the concept of a data-driven, structured performance partnering methodology excels. The **MP3 Model (Methodology, Planning, Process, Performance Management)** represents the first comprehensive approach to structured partner seller performance turning the channel into a production line feeding new opportunities for co-sell and resell. MP3 is designed to address the systemic challenges of the traditional program-centric unstructured partner sales model integrating with any sales methodology. Our approach enhances the traditional partnership framework with the level of visibility and control typically found only in direct sales, effectively merging the strengths of both models.

MP3 defines an innovative system to help revenue leaders structure their partnership models to deliver on the promise of predictable revenue growth. Channel Force introduces the first end-to-end Sales Acceleration and ChannelOps system focused on achieving Profitable Efficient Growth (PEG). This book will define the problems with today's partnering models and walk you through a process to help you organize, educate, equip, and deliver a new structured performance model to achieve your desired revenue goals. We will demonstrate how to transform your partner ecosystem into a powerful source of revenue, employing precision and discipline - much like that of a contemporary production line. This involves managing Inputs (active sellers), the Production Process (sales acceleration), and Outputs (new pipeline). Additionally, we will explore how ChannelOps and new channel sales mathematics serve as vital system controls to oversee this sales production line's efficiency identifying issues and trends to manage outputs.

This book embarks on a journey to explore the ever-evolving world of partnerships in the digital age. It offers a comprehensive guide for both beginners and seasoned professionals, unveiling strategies and best practices to unlock the true potential of partner-sourced sales acceleration turning your partner ecosystem into a finely tuned revenue-producing engine.

MP3- Structured Performance Engine

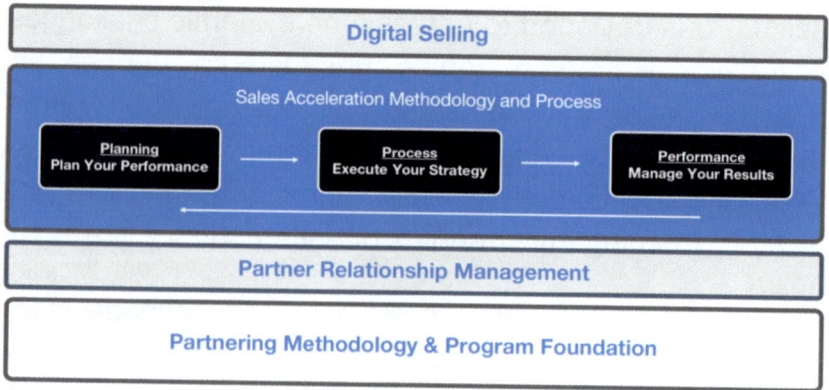

Here's what you can expect to gain:

- **Insights**: Discover the latest trends and insights shaping the partnership landscape, and learn how to adapt and thrive in a rapidly changing environment.

- **Strategies**: Gain access to proven strategies for developing, managing, and optimizing partner sales performance, whether you are a vendor, a partner, or an ecosystem builder.

- **Data-Driven Approach:** Learn how to harness the power of data and structured performance to drive results, measure success, and maximize Return on Investment (ROI) in your partnerships.

- **Actionable Advice:** Find practical, actionable advice and step-by-step guidance to implement sales acceleration strategies that work for your specific business needs.

Reader Journey (What to Expect)

As you embark on this journey through the pages of this book, it's important to understand how to make the most of the content:

- **Foundational Knowledge:** Chapters 1-3 are foundational chapters that lay the groundwork for understanding the importance of structured partner-led sales creation orchestration in the digital age.

- **Progressive Learning:** Each chapter builds upon the previous one, providing a progressive learning experience that takes you from the basics to advanced strategies.

- **Actionable Insights:** In Chapters 4-9 you'll find practical insights and actionable steps that you can implement immediately to enhance your sales creation efforts.

- **Reference and Resource:** Use this book as a reference guide, returning to specific chapters and sections as needed to refresh your knowledge or address specific challenges.

As you turn the pages, keep in mind that partnerships are not a one-size-fits-all endeavor. Your unique journey in the world of partner-sourced sales acceleration will be shaped by your industry, goals, and organizational context. This book aims to equip you with the knowledge, tools, and inspiration needed to build a next-generation partner-sourced revenue engine that consistently produces results.

So, let's embark on this journey together, as we explore the future of ecosystem GTM models, the need for structured performance, and the boundless opportunities that partnerships offer in the new digital age.

If you google sales methodologies, more than sixteen different sales systems are returned for results. As you can see, sales training, skills development, and process alignment constitute a significant industry. One of the initial steps for revenue leadership is to align the sales team around a unified selling approach. Companies strive to standardize processes that not only enhance their performance but also ensure a cohesive approach across their sales teams. The adoption of a sales methodology serves as the blueprint that guides sales professionals through structured processes from prospecting to closing deals. In addition, sales methodologies at the company level create a system of inputs (RevOps) and processes (sales process), that produce predictable outputs (revenue). This standardization is vital for businesses aiming to streamline their sales operations, improve efficiency, and achieve consistent revenue results.

Standardization Produces Results

As RevOps gains significance, companies are broadening their metrics beyond just top-line revenue, focusing instead on measuring Profitable Efficient Growth (PEG). PEG is a novel RevOps metric that goes beyond simply tracking top-line revenue and the expenses incurred to achieve it. PEG measures the resources needed to attain these financial outcomes, providing a more comprehensive assessment of operational efficiency. The reason companies standardize a common approach to selling is simple: it's a primary tool to deliver consistent revenue growth! Sales structure and process help companies deliver better results at a lower cost with better efficiency. Additionally, standardization provides:

- **Consistency and Predictability-** A standardized sales methodology ensures that all sales representatives approach sales scenarios in a consistent manner, fostering a level of predictability in both sales outcomes and forecasts. This uniformity helps in setting clear expectations for performance and outcomes, making it easier to identify areas of improvement and success.

- **Improved Sales Performance-** A well-defined sales methodology equips sales teams with a structured approach to selling, which can significantly enhance their ability to close deals. By following a proven framework, sales representatives navigate the sales process more effectively, from identifying leads to successfully converting them into customers.

- **Effective Training and Onboarding-** For new sales representatives, a standardized sales methodology serves as a valuable learning tool. It provides a clear framework and process to follow, which can accelerate the onboarding process and help new hires become productive quickly.

- **Better Sales Analytics and Forecasting-** When sales teams follow a standardized methodology, it becomes easier to track and analyze sales data. This uniform data collection enables more accurate sales forecasting and analytics, providing insights into what strategies are working and which areas need improvement.

Popular Sales Methodology Examples

Choosing the right sales methodology (system) for your

organization is a crucial step toward the goal of profitable efficient revenue growth. However, selecting the best approach isn't always easy. Each methodology comes with its own set of advantages and disadvantages. Understanding your buyer's journey, the complexity of your sales process, and the skill level of your sales teams play an important role in helping guide a company to the best process for its needs. Several sales methodologies have gained popularity for their effectiveness in SaaS and Technology. These methodologies include but are not limited to:

- **SPIN Selling:** Focuses on identifying the Situation, Problem, Implication, and Need-payoff, helping sales reps better understand and address customer needs.

- **MEDDIC:** Stands for Metrics, Economic Buyer, Decision Criteria, Decision Process, Identify Pain, and Champion, focusing on qualifying leads to ensure they are worth pursuing.

- **Winning By Design:** Focuses on a systematic, customer-centric approach to sales that emphasizes building sustainable relationships rather than just closing short-term deals. It uses a structured framework to align sales processes with the customer's buying journey, ensuring a more consistent and predictable sales performance.

Companies often adopt popular methodologies due to their widespread acceptance, proven effectiveness, simplicity of implementing training, and ease of system integration.

The Need for A Partner Sales Methodology

While there are numerous effective sales methodologies, a specific partnering methodology that defines a structured sales acceleration process is notably absent. There's no common partner-sourced sales creation system available today. Traditionally, partnering organizations receive training alongside direct sellers using the company's existing selling model. Although beneficial, this approach does not fully address the unique challenges of indirect sales, where companies utilize third-party partners. There's a clear need for a specialized partner sales methodology that focuses on developing the necessary skills and processes to cultivate partnerships to generate new business. In today's complex partnering world, every channel organization needs a structured performance process tailored to transition passive sellers into proactive demand creators. This partner selling methodology should enhance any sales process, offering a framework that enables partners to actively develop new sales resulting in significant revenue growth.

New Partnering System Requirements

Partnership models are an obvious sales strategy to deliver on the promise of profitable efficient revenue growth. However, the partnering process currently has a significant gap. The industry urgently needs a systematic, performance-based sales methodology to organize the partner demand creation process. Our industry needs a structured partner sales pipeline process to complement the direct sales approaches used today. This new partner-led pipeline system must be compatible with, and enhance, the vendors adopted sales process. Establishing a structured partner sales creation model will:

1. Turn passive partners into proactive participants in the sales process.

2. Emphasize and incentivize the importance of prospecting, account coverage and sales development in the context of partner-led selling.

3. Deliver predictable, profitable, efficient revenue growth.

SALES METHODOLOGIES ARE SYSTEMS!

Structured sales acceleration partnering produces these benefits:

- **Empowers Partners:** Equips partners with the tools and framework to actively engage with prospects, creating demand from the ground up.

- **Enhances Partner Enablement:** Provides a systematic approach for partners to identify and qualify leads, ensuring they focus their efforts on high-potential opportunities.

- **Complements Existing Sales Processes**: Augments your current sales methodology with a front-end process that integrates seamlessly with your established sales practices.

- **Creates Active Sellers:** Transitions passive sellers into proactive lead generators delivering results to improve co-sell operations.

- **Creates Account & Market Coverage:** Identifies account coverage and engagement gaps leading to well-defined territory plans and better buyer engagement.

This strategic alignment between sales methodology and its channel sales operations is crucial for for companies relying on indirect sales channels to deliver revenue growth.

While the benefits of a standardized partner sales methodology are clear, the technology industry has yet to develop a universal approach. This lack of structured performance is primarily due to the focus on partnership performance rather than on individual partner sellers' (Account Managers) performance. Companies prioritize developing partner programs, ecosystems, and sales enablement aiming to boost partner sales activities. However, the go-to-market process for partner sellers remains largely ad hoc, and opportunistic, which hinders the standardization of a partner sales methodology.

Defining a standard partner sales methodology offers numerous benefits beyond the obvious better sales performance and greater commissions for sellers. A partnering sales system elevates the partnering function from a sales support role to a strategic component of the business. A next-generation partner sales methodology will solve many of the core issues with today's best effort GTM models providing a direct line of visibility from sales strategy to partner execution to revenue outcomes with clear attribution. This clarity and focus allow for a more streamlined and simplified partnering function, reducing complexity and enhancing sales efficiency. By adopting a standardized process, organizations can ensure consistency across all partner engagements, which creates more effective performance management.

A structured sales performance process moves partnering away from the unpredictable "partner and pray" models to a more reliable and systematic method of managing and measuring partner contributions. Overall, a next-generation partner sales methodology not only enhances the profitability and effectiveness of partner channels but also aligns partner activities directly with the company's broader sales and business objectives.

Having discussed the advantages of a systematic partnering methodology, let's now turn our attention to the existing partnering model to pinpoint its challenges. This analysis will help us develop our structured, partner-led sales creation methodology that addresses these issues effectively.

Chapter Application

Companies understand the significant benefits that a structured sales methodology brings. In fact, one of the initial actions a new Chief Revenue Officer (CRO) often takes is to assess the sales methodology to ensure it aligns with the required skill level and selling style for the companies solutions. Sales methodologies establish logical workflows and productivity processes just like a production line. In fact, Sales organizations are designed as production lines, with inputs (sales resources), a production process (sales methodology), system controls (customer relationship management tools), and outputs (sales). For companies with market-leading solutions and structured sales processes, sales productivity can be controlled by adjusting the number of salespeople and the accounts covered that the company decides to invest in.

However, this structured approach has traditionally been lacking in the partnering model. The partner model was never designed with the necessary inputs, processes, and controls to systematically create a new pipeline. There has been no common partner-sourced revenue creation methodology that aligns with the partner community to deliver profitable, efficient revenue growth. This represents the most significant gap in today's partner model.

The takeaway from this chapter is clear: we need a structured performance model that creates proactive sellers and maximizes the performance of the partner ecosystem. By implementing such a model, companies can ensure that partner-driven sales are as systematic and productive as direct sales, fostering a more dynamic and effective partner network.

TODAY'S PARTNERING MODEL CHALLENGES

2

Over the last decade, the partnership sector has witnessed significant innovation. Jay McBain, a leading channel analyst from Canalys and a top industry authority, releases an annual overview mapping the channel ecosystem. This map categorizes companies into 11 different channel solution areas. In 2023, the map featured 233 companies, an increase of 38 from the previous year. These companies span a wide range of disciplines, including learning, data management, recruiting, marketing automation, marketplace integration, ecosystem management, and incentives management to name a few. Collectively, these channel ecosystem services companies generated over $5 billion in revenue in 2022 and continue to grow. (Canalys Channel Ecosystem Landscape Report 2023)

The channel ecosystem services and technology industry is tackling some of the biggest issues associated with channels and is improving the efficiency of the traditional opportunistic fulfillment model. But as famed management guru, Peter Drucker, once said, "There's nothing more useless than doing efficiently that which should not be done at all." It is our thesis that improvements in technologies will only help a company be marginally more efficient (time) but may not make the organization significantly more productive (greater revenue). To significantly improve partner-sourced revenue, the underlying model must change.

The growth in the channel ecosystem technology and services industry can largely be attributed to addressing the shortcomings of traditional partnering process and shifts in technology and consumption models. These shortcomings and shifts are changing the way consumers research, purchase, and utilize technology. As technology modernizes and consumption models evolve, they are challenging the structure, processes and performance of the traditional opportunistic fulfillment models of the 1980s. Such changes are driving a necessary transformation in partnership strategies to generate the performance levels required for sustained partner-sourced revenue growth. There is an urgent need for a more innovative process to tackle the issues stemming from the current unstructured partner sales approach. Although channel ecosystem technology and services companies are making laudable strides in offering innovative solutions to these common challenges, it raises an important question:

Are we solving the core issue or just treating symptoms?

This book's processes, and methodologies are based on a belief that the opportunistic go-to-market element of the program-centric partnering model is fundamentally flawed. Opportunistic sales models (reactive partner fulfillment) lead to underperforming partnerships, tepid vendor reception within the partner community, and an expensive channel model that diminishes Return on Investment.

The fundamental flaw of the opportunistic partner sales model lies in the unstructured sales creation process that occurs between partner sellers and the target market. In the latter stages of our program-centric model, partner sales efforts are sporadic and based more on chance than strategy and structure. Lacking a structured playbook and clear sales creation processes, partner sellers often resort to passive fulfillment tactics, passively waiting for opportunities rather than actively generating new demand. The primary issue with these traditional models is their disproportionate focus on partner programs at the expense of empowering structured demand-creation processes that actively facilitate new sales. The go-to-market strategy is a crucial component of our partnering model, essential for driving and sustaining revenue growth. Instead of minor adjustments to the partner program, the priority should be to develop structured GTM sales creation processes with our partners that promote proactive selling behaviors and well-defined target market coverage. In my view, many recent innovations in the partnering process focus more on managing performance symptoms, such as improving efficiency, rather than addressing the root cause: unstructured sales processes and passive partner engagements.

To illustrate, let's walk through the traditional program-centric partnering model and identify the go-to-market problems that limit the model's effectiveness.

As we progress through the chapter, I will build the case for a new structured performance revenue creation process. Before we begin, I want to make it clear that I am not dismissing the value of partner programs and traditional workflows. They are foundational to a successful partnering process. However, I will examine the go-to-market elements of the model to highlight its flaws so we can innovate and build a better model. Looking at the typical program-centric workflow in Figure 1, the steps of the typical program-centric model follow a logical flow:

Figure 1.

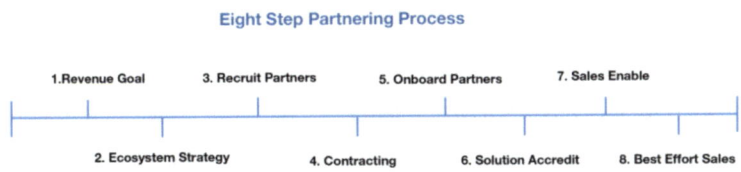

Common Sales Creation Workflow

Eight Step Partnering Process

1.Revenue Goal	3. Recruit Partners	5. Onboard Partners	7. Sales Enable
2. Ecosystem Strategy	4. Contracting	6. Solution Accredit	8. Best Effort Sales

Program-Centric Model is a Partner Focused Priority Model

- **Revenue Goal:** The partner model process begins with setting a revenue target or quota that the company aims to achieve.

- **Ecosystem Strategy:** The company crafts a strategy for its partnerships, specifying the types of partnerships, resource allocations, enablement process, and marketing plans to meet the revenue goal.

- **Recruit Partners:** Partners are recruited to expand market coverage and enhance sales activities with each solution's target market.

- **Contracting:** Establishing the legal frameworks necessary for conducting business.

- **Onboard Partners:** Once partners are signed, they undergo development to align with the company's partner program standards. Concurrently, joint business plans are created to structure incentives, selling efforts, and solution support activities, providing a framework to monitor partnership progress.

- **Solution Accredit**: Partners' sales personnel and engineers receive training on the solution's value propositions, features, competitive advantages, positioning, and technical design and support.

- **Sales Enable**: Partners are equipped with marketing collateral and integrated into a targeted account planning process to leverage their existing customer base for new sales.

- **Best-Effort Selling**: Partner sellers mine their base of customers or engage in bidding for opportunities when prompted by potential customers or vendors.

This sequence presents a structured workflow designed to enhance the effectiveness of partner programs in meeting specific business goals. While this model appears sound on the surface, its program-centric nature poses challenges to efficient revenue creation. This workflow focuses on recruiting and scaling partnerships to build market coverage but leaves sales creation to each partner to address using their own GTM process. Although partner leaders have improved support for partners in this area, we have yet to address a universal methodology for structured partner performance. The absence of a structured approach to partner sales creation represents a significant gap in every partnering model. We have yet to develop a cohesive partner sales methodology that efficiently generates a new sales pipeline to feed our co-sell engine.

To further highlight the issues with program-centric models, consider the following challenges:

1. The current partnering model doesn't yield predictable revenue growth.

2. It's challenging to achieve consistent partner sales performance and cultivate proactive partner sales managers who consistently develop new opportunities
3. Requires continuously recruiting new partners and cycling out low performers, leading to higher costs and a reduced return on investment.

It's illogical to think the solution to the passive partner sales manager problem is to recruit more partners in the hope of creating more proactive sellers. This is an outdated mindset. The solution is to fix the passive seller problem with structured performance.

Program-Centric Flip Phone

Think of today's program-centric model as the old flip phone. Most of us can remember the days when flip phones were all the rage. We could make calls, send texts, and even listen to music. They came equipped with a few extra features like a basic calculator and GPS. The average flip phone significantly enhanced our daily lives, both personally and professionally. We were quite content with our flip phones—until the smartphone came along. Once we experienced the capabilities of a smartphone, with its full screen, internet connectivity, and app functionalities, the flip phone quickly became obsolete. The transition to smartphones happened overnight and revolutionized how we integrate technology into every aspect of our lives.

So, why bring up the story of flip phones? It parallels where we stand with our partnering model evolution. We're currently operating with the equivalent of a flip phone in a world where the smartphone exists. The flip phone has limitations that are addressed by the smartphone. Let's look at the limitations of the program-centric partnering model. So, we can address these issues when we build a better model.

Unstructured Sales Creation Limitations

Here are four key areas of the opportunistic partner sales model that require updates to modernize the approach. These limitations represent fundamental challenges that every new partnering methodology must address.

One: No Predictable Revenue

As you can see, the typical partnering model is a process or sequential workflow to recruit, onboard, accredit, develop, and scale partnerships to revenue growth; it's a sequence of tasks and operations designed to produce an outcome, compliant partners to the partner program and fairness in the market between partner sellers. The common partnering process has its place and provides several benefits, but the traditional partnering model lacks the key elements needed to produce a systematic approach to revenue creation. The traditional partnering model lacks production planning, a structured partner-seller production process, and systems controls to manage revenue outcomes. In other words, the current process doesn't produce predictable revenue outcomes.

Two: Results In Passive Sellers

Looking at the opportunistic program-centric approach to leverage in Figure 2, there's an imbalance of priorities. In this model, the emphasis is on recruiting partners and molding them to fit the standards of a partner program. Conversely, the channel model focuses on ensuring fairness for partners and rewarding them based on their commitment and performance to the program. At the sales level, partnership sellers and pre-sales engineers are equipped with product-specific knowledge, value propositions, and a broad understanding of business and technical use cases and value propositions. The theory posits that incentives and product knowledge enhance the perceived value of a solution, thereby encouraging proactive sales behavior. In other words, partner sellers focus on selling what they know and are incentivized to sell. However, if these sellers are not adequately prepared for success, a single failed attempt at positioning your solution may lead them to abandon it and shift to selling other solutions, ultimately becoming passive sellers.

Figure. 2

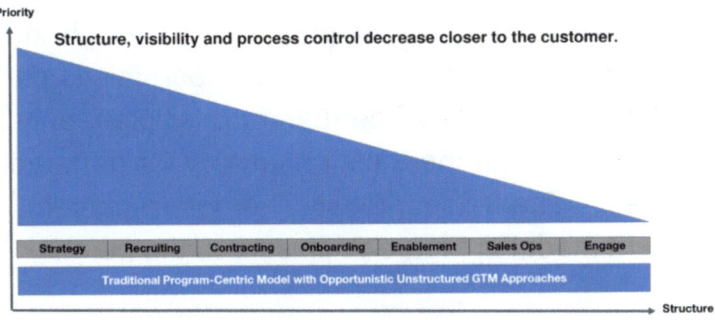

The problem becomes apparent as we move through the stages of partner development: strategy, recruiting, contracting, onboarding, enablement, sales operations, and customer engagement. The further partners progress through the workflow, partners often find themselves with dwindling resources, sporadic support, and less structure. Consequently, the burden of prospecting and selling falls squarely on the partners, who often must navigate prospecting independently of the vendor. Without a structured approach to prospecting that produces easy-to-achieve results, partner sellers' default to opportunistic sales behaviors chasing deals that are created by someone else. Furthermore, in the programmatic channel partnership model, partners frequently end up functioning as order takers, springing into action only when prompted by a quote request. This leads to the prevalent 80/20 rule in partnerships, where a minority of partners generate most of the revenue, creating a continuous cycle of recruiting new partners to find high-performance partnerships to create sales growth.

Three: No Systematic Sales Creation

The traditional opportunistic program-centric partnering model emphasizes solution value and incentives to motivate the partner community towards proactive sales behavior. The prevailing theory holds that higher incentives for a solution will prioritize its sale. While this generally holds true, fostering sales activity requires more than just incentives—it necessitates making the sales creation straightforward through structured GTM processes and sales plays. The opportunistic partnering model, which operates on free market principles, only loosely provides partners with the tools necessary for generating new opportunities. The opportunistic program-centric market development model in Figure 3. illustrates the point.

Figure 3.

Program-Centric Market Development Model

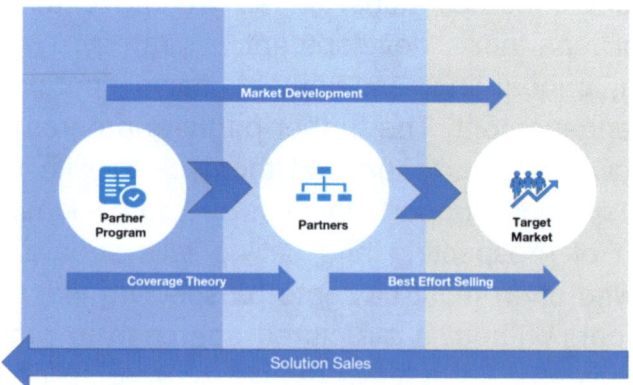

This is a simplistic view of the common GTM process of today's channel representing the Partner Program, Partners, and Solution Target Markets. In this illustration, The **Market Development Line** represents the vendor's efforts in cultivating the market for their solutions with their target audience. The goal is to create market awareness and preference, generating inbound leads that partners, sales, and marketing can address. This encompasses investments in marketing, market development, and sales to enhance recognition of the value of your solution among your target market.

The **Coverage Theory Line** represents the vendor's partner recruiting process, which posits that recruiting more partners in theory will increase market coverage, create active sellers, and generate better sales and revenue results. For hot products with great market demand, Coverage Theory works because partner sellers prioritize selling the easiest most profitable solutions to sell. However, solutions that demand more effort from the partner community to sell require significantly higher investments in sales enablement and incentives to yield results. This is because relying solely on partners' best efforts tends to be inefficient and often necessitates a large partner network to generate the volume of active sellers needed to scale revenue growth effectively.

The program-centric partner model is based on best-effort selling. The **Best Effort Selling Line** symbolizes the opportunistic sales efforts from the partner community, which operates without a structured strategy from the vendor for generating new sales. Many partner sellers reactively engage customers in an ad hoc fashion, engaging when either the vendor or the customer defines an opportunity.

As you can see, the program-centric model lacks systematic sales acceleration, planning, and prospecting at the partner seller and account level. The opportunistic nature of partner sales is creating inefficient account coverage and revenue underperformance.

Four: Produces Core Partnering Challenges

Best-effort selling, the absence of revenue planning, and a structured sales acceleration framework pose significant challenges for revenue leaders. Furthermore, the lack of strategy execution visibility creates a challenge to align partner sales strategy execution with actual results (attribution). Almost every partner leader is struggling with how to address the fundamental issues stemming from opportunistic partnering models that lack a structured sales creation system. See Figure 4.

Figure 4.

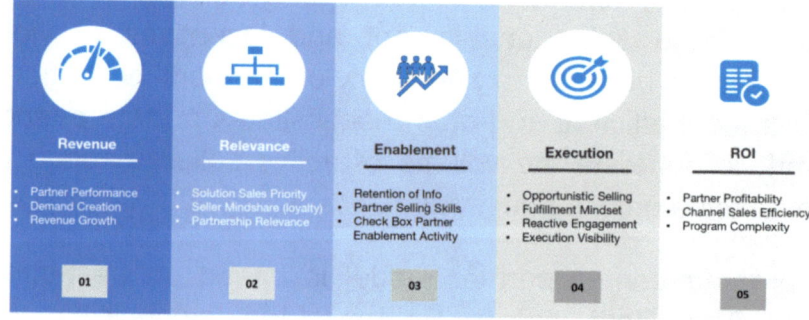

The core challenges associated with every opportunistic partnering model include:

- **Revenue Growth** - Given that 80% of channel revenue typically comes from 20% of partners, how can the distribution be adjusted to engage a larger number of partners to contribute consistently and predictably to revenue growth?

- **Partnership Relevance** - How can the importance that

partners place on selling my solution be enhanced to foster better engagement, mindshare, and loyalty, thereby increasing the number of active sellers?

- **Strategy Enablement** - Is it possible to equip our partners with the sales skills needed to effectively identify, develop, and close new sales? Can we improve information retention and build better sales strategy and solution competency?

- **Sales Execution** - How can we improve the sales funnel and win rates among our partners? Furthermore, how can we gain visibility to sales strategy execution and prospecting activity to boost partner seller effectiveness?

- **Partner Model ROI** - What steps can be taken to enhance the sales efficiency of our partners? Can we increase time-to-value, and improve engagement rates, win rates, and average deal sizes, leading to lower levels of effort and improved profitability?

These fundamental issues stem from unstructured partner sales philosophies inherent in the program-centric model. The best-effort selling philosophy of the model fosters these problems, contributing to the short average tenure of a channel leader, which is typically only 18-24 months. The common "partner & pray" approach with opportunistic sales creation is largely ineffective for solutions with low market awareness and demand. While the ecosystem services industry is developing innovative solutions to mitigate the symptoms of our core issues, the underlying cause — the absence of a structured performance methodology — remains unaddressed. Companies need to evolve their opportunistic partnering models by integrating a structured performance methodology, bringing much-needed balance and effectiveness to their partnership strategies.

Chapter Application

While I recognize the value of the program-centric partnering model and commend many of you for successfully mastering the model, a critical assessment of its underlying efficiency and performance reveals substantial opportunities for improvement. Honestly, the widely accepted 80/20 rule, which often defines success within traditional partner models, would be deemed unacceptable in nearly any other context. For example, a 20% success rate translates to a failing grade on a test, a low batting average, or a poor shooting percentage in sports, etcetera.

Today, companies are trying to address revenue, relevance, and ROI issues with better technology, revamped partner programs, processes, and structured partner coverage. For example, Microsoft overtook Apple in value by recognizing the seven partners surrounding each customer and changing its programs, processes, and technology to execute. While this model is clearly producing results, could they have improved the efficiency and cost structure of their partnering model with a structured performance methodology, delivering better results with fewer partners?

The partnering model must address profitable efficient growth! It's time for us to reexamine our partnering model with fresh eyes and consider a new approach. Adopting a methodology that incorporates structured performance principles, will significantly enhance the effectiveness of our partnerships and improce sales efficiency.

CROs and Partner Pros, are you experiencing any of the challenges associated with the opportunistic go-to-market practices associated with partner sales? Recognizing the limitations of this common approach is crucial, especially the need for a structured performance model that effectively

25

addresses the final stages of the partner-to-market sales process. Understanding these constraints allows you to better identify and tackle the fundamental issues hindering your partner models effectiveness. To start the process of addressing these challenges, here are a few actionable steps:

- **Assess Your Current Model:** Evaluate your current partnership GTM model against the traditional opportunistic fulfillment models discussed. Identify whether your approach aligns more with program-centric approaches or structured revenue growth.

- **Embrace Structured GTM Strategies:** Be willing to shift your focus from tweaking your partner programs to incorporating a comprehensive structured performance go-to-market (GTM) process that structures your partner sellers prospecting activities.

- **Innovate Beyond the Status Quo:** Inspired by the analogy of smartphones replacing flip phones, consider how your partnership model can evolve beyond traditional methods to incorporate newer, more effective strategies and technologies that meet current market demands.

Having recognized the limitations of the traditional opportunistic partnering model, don't accept the status quo, victory favors the bold! Let's begin introducing our structured performance methodology, MP3. Our model has been architected to address the foundational issues plaguing today's channel model and aims to generate substantial revenue growth more cost-effectively than the conventional program-centric approach.

INTRODUCTION TO
STRUCTURED PERFORMANCE

3

Leverage: the power to influence a person or situation to achieve a particular outcome. - Dictionary.com

We have covered many of the core challenges with today's partnering models. The solution to these challenges is structured performance. The next frontier in channel innovation involves adopting structured sales acceleration models with next-generation ChannelOps planning. Figure 5. Outlines the evolution of partnering models to Structured Performance models. As businesses intensify their efforts to increase revenue and cut costs, the opportunistic program-centric partner model is increasingly under scrutiny. A significant gap in our current partnering approach needs to be addressed, the absence of a standardized partner sales creation methodology. A new methodology must align vendors and partners around a unified front-end pipeline process to generate better sales efficiency and performance. This process evolution will focus on planning sales performance and resourcing sales execution to make selling solutions easier more efficient and profitable for sellers. This new methodology will equip partner sellers with the structure and the selling skills necessary to target, develop, and close new sales faster and with less effort to produce the lead. The next level of innovation transforms the partner go-to-market process into a production line system of proactive seller inputs, structured selling processes, and performance management resulting in new pipeline outputs. This new approach requires new principles and a better leverage model to develop a structured performance revenue engine.

Figure 5.

Partner Model Life-Cycles & Evolution

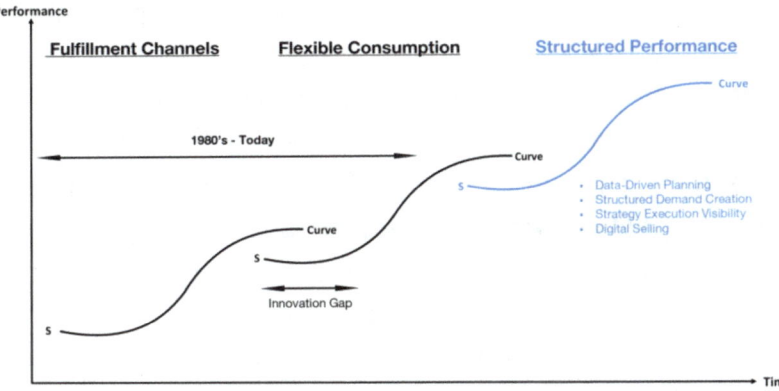

Leverage Models And Structured Performance

Here's the big secret! The key to delivering partner-sourced revenue growth isn't increasing the number of new partners you recruit; it's increasing the number of proactive partner sales managers and economic buyer engagements you're partnering GTM model produces. It's easy to lose sight of the fact that partner programs are designed for one primary purpose: to produce leverage and ultimately create active sellers. Active sellers, in turn, are empowered to generate sales. Thought leaders such as Jared Fuller, author of Nearbound, and Bob Moore, author of Ecosystem Led Growth, grasp this concept well. They have developed better go-to-market models that help partners and vendors enhance engagements with economic buyers. Their books, which I highly recommend, offer valuable insights into crafting superior leverage models that produce demand-creation activity.

Creating leverage is the secret to generating proactive behavior. In fact, the entire partnering process is designed with the purpose of creating leverage to generate proactive sellers. This chapter takes a deeper look at leverage models and what we need to do differently to improve our leverage models to increase the number of proactive sellers our models produce. My goal is to provide a fresh perspective on partner seller influence. It's crucial to examine the program-centric model of creating leverage using discounts, margins, and incentives to influence outcomes. This model is effective in scenarios where there is strong market demand for solutions, high margins, limited competition, and a focus on selling high-cost capital expenditure items. However, with the shift towards software and subscription-based consumption models and changes in partner compensation structures, the program-centric leverage model needs help to adapt.

To overcome the shortcomings of the traditional leverage model, we need to explore enhancements that align with today's sellers, current market conditions, and technological advancements.

Our revised leverage model operates on a clear principle: **Individual Sellers are motivated to lead with solutions that are both easy, efficient and profitable to sell**. In other words, Sales Managers are inclined to sell what benefits them the most and what takes the least amount of effort to produce a win. Therefore, our leverage strategy must extend beyond performance-based incentives to make it easier for sellers at every stage of the sales cycle. This approach incorporating structured selling techniques with playbooks and introducing activity-based rewards, such as meeting incentives.

Modern leverage models must strike a balance between the effort required to develop a new sale and the incentives that motivate sellers to actively prospect. To establish this new leverage model, companies must embrace and apply new principles that better fit the motivations of today's partner sellers.

New Principle: To maximize partner-sourced revenue growth, structured selling is required.

"Structured selling is the new leverage model." Structured selling makes it easier, efficient and highly profitable for sellers to proactively prospect. So what exactly is structured selling? Structured selling utilizes data, revenue planning, scripted prospecting processes, planned targeted account coverage, and clearly defined sales development processes tailored to each stage of the buyer's journey to generate new leads. Additionally, it includes activity-based incentives and rigorous performance management of the entire selling process. See Figure 6.

Adopting a structured performance model significantly transforms the partner-sourced revenue process, yielding several key benefits:

- **Improves Revenue Performance:** Structured performance transforms passive fulfillment partners into active sellers, significantly boosting top-of-funnel performance, improving win rates, and increasing revenue.

- **Increases Relevance:** Structured selling makes selling easier and profitable for sellers providing a step-by-step demand creation recipe that fosters brand loyalty and improves mindshare.

- **Improves ROI:** Structured performance enhances win rates, increases deal sizes, and yields predictable sales outcomes. Implementing a structured prospecting methodology boosts sales efficiency and reduces the cost of sales.

Figure 6.

New Partner Seller Leverage Model

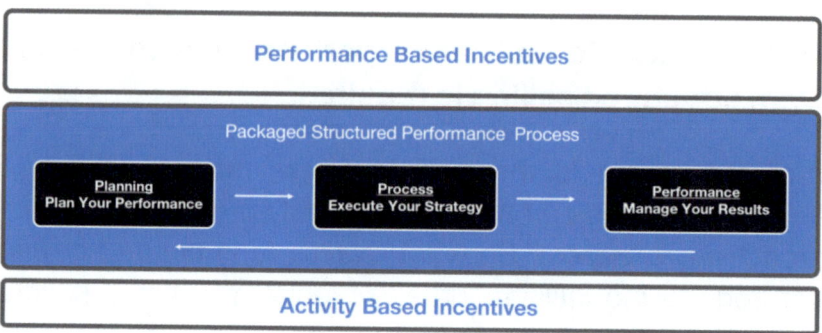

Ultimately, implementing a structured performance model addresses our five core opportunistic sales model issues by enhancing revenue performance, increasing partner relevance and mindshare, resolving enablement and execution visibility challenges, and delivering improved ROI.

Structured Performance Vs Program-Centric

Adopting a structured performance model can profoundly transform your traditional program-centric partnering model. Figure 7 illustrates the distinctions between these approaches, showcasing how structured performance shifts away from the opportunistic nature of program-centric models. This shift brings numerous benefits, enhancing the performance, visibility, and efficiency of the partner sales process. These modifications lead to a more effective partner GTM process. Additionally, these shifts reorient the partnering model to function more like a manufacturing production line, offering a systematic approach to market coverage, sales acceleration, enablement, and other key areas. This alignment enhances efficiency and effectiveness across the board.

Figure 7.

Program-Centric vs Structured Performance

Category	Program-Centric	Structured Performance	Benefits
Channel Theory	• Best Effort Demand Creation	• Structured Sales Creation.	Creates structured coverage improving channel management and revenue performance.
Enablement Focus	• Products, Programs, & Certification	• Selling & Demand Creation.	Creates active partners sellers significantly improving 20/80 active/passive mix.
Sales Model	• Opportunistic Fulfillment	• Partner Led Market Development	Improves channel efficiency, coverage, and win rates.
Coverage Model	• Geography	• Target Accounts	Provides actionable coverage and improves strategy execution.
Partner Planning	• Business Plans (Partnership)	• Data-Driven, Execution Plans	Creates an actionable and measurable sales strategy and execution plan to improve results.
Channel Marketing	• General Marketing Collateral	• Customized Sales Plays	Creates impactful targeted messaging improving the probability of engagement.
Data Capture	• Statistical ERP (POS & Trends)	• Partner Seller Activity	Actionable data capture and dashboards provide visibility to partner seller, strategy execution.
Revenue Modeling	• Limited Modeling	• Performance Benchmarking	Allows for performance management of the channel to create predictable and improved results.
Dashboards	• Historical Partner Performance	• Real-time Strategy Execution	End-to-end visibility of seller strategy execution allowing for attribution!
Performance Reports	• Program Metrics (Limited)	• Active Sellers Activity	Answers how (?) the partner achieved the performance result.

Structured performance models rebalance the priorities of the program-centric model. Here's how a sales-centric partnering model operates in comparison with traditional partnering approaches:

- **Shifts Priorities:** The emphasis moves away from managing partner programs to creating partner sellers who actively prospect for new opportunities.

- **Structured Performance Over Opportunism:** We prioritize systematic prospecting and account coverage rather than relying on opportunistic sales fulfillment.

- **Strategy Enablement:** Transitioning from basic product-focused enablement to strategic execution, teaching partner sellers how to effectively execute your solution's sales strategy and prospecting process.

- **Redefining Coverage:** Partner coverage shifts from geographic to focusing on accounts and relationship scores, targeting where partners can be most effective.

- **Refined Performance Metrics:** Moving from broad partner-level metrics to more specific active seller metrics and detailed account engagements.

- **Enhanced Visibility:** Transitioning from deal registration to using account engagement data for clearer insights into partner execution.

- **Integration of New Tools:** Digital selling platforms and intelligent buyer journey solutions are used to enhance partner outreach and target account mapping.

- **Predictable Revenue Planning:** Forecasting and point of sale (POS) data are augmented with tools that enhance revenue predictability.

- **Replacing the 80/20 Rule:** The focus shifts to nurturing active sellers rather than continually recruiting new partners, aiming for a broader base of effective contributors.

- **Efficiency and Cost-effectiveness:** Leveraging active sellers achieves quicker time-to-value and reduces costs compared to the continual recruitment of new partners.

These changes underline a comprehensive complement to the traditional partnering model, making it more aligned with current market demands and technological advancements. Maximizing partner sales performance requires adopting a "Data-Driven Structured Performance" approach. We are moving away from the traditional "partner and pray" unstructured selling models to a more methodical, data-informed strategy that structures, organizes, and directs partner go-to-market performance. The strategy for creating partner demand will no longer rely solely on your partner program and incentives. Instead, it will be seamlessly integrated with a broader company selling sales strategy, marking a significant shift in enablement focus from program-centric to strategically empowered. Structured Performance models necessitate a deeper level of enablement, commitment and co-sell alignment. By equipping partners with a clearly articulated demand creation plan and process, companies greatly increase the likelihood that a larger number of partner sellers will proactively prospect and generate new demand.

MP3 Model Introduction

To address the challenges of opportunistic partner-centric models, Channel Force Inc. has developed a comprehensive structured performance methodology, MP3! MP3 represents the four phases required to build partner-powered structured performance revenue engines. The process is outlined in Figure 8. Here is a high-level introduction:

■ **Methodology-** Our methodology is a foundational GTM solution planning process designed to maximize sales performance for solutions when sold through partners. Our solution GTM planning methodology is based on a five-phase Indirect Sales Acceleration Model (ISAM). ISAM includes assessments, strategy profiles, solution empowerment, partner enablement, and strategy execution resourcing. Our ISAM Model marks the first data-driven approach to sales acceleration planning. Our model develops the essential plans, processes and resources needed to convert passive partners into a dynamic sales production line capable of generating substantial sales pipeline outputs.

■ **Planning-** Incorporating precise revenue planning metrics is essential for sustained revenue growth. Our revenue planning process is a first of its kind RevOps channel revenue planning model. Our innovative planning process identifies the necessary sales and prospecting metrics for each territory and partner to achieve their revenue goals.

34

These metrics outline the inputs needed for our sales production line process. This revenue planning enables the creation of actionable territory and partner execution plans, allowing channel managers and partners to not only meet but exceed their revenue targets.

Our Planning IQ application calculates survey inputs to establish sales performance metrics, key performance indicators (KPIs), actions, activities, and timeframes crucial for exceeding performance benchmarks. Our planning tools facilitate the development of detailed revenue plans, grounded in defined revenue roadmap metrics. Data-driven revenue represents a groundbreaking innovation, extending the RevOps process into the channel model, enhancing strategic planning. With the MP3 Planning Process revenue goals and partner plans are coupled with revenue plans that guide activities and timeframes required to achieve the numbers. The MP3-Planning process defines the inputs for our production line sales acceleration process.

- **Process-** Every system needs to process inputs to create the desired output. The MP3 framework utilizes a packaged sales acceleration process to turn prospecting activity into new demand. Our sales acceleration model incorporates a comprehensive prospecting process that includes advanced target account planning, structured coverage models, structured prospecting processes, and strategy resourcing, making it one of the most comprehensive partner-led demand creation methodologies available today. MP3 also provides options to integrate advanced technologies, such as artificial intelligence (AI) driven prospecting technologies and digital selling platforms to align with the modern buyer's journey. By focusing on sales plays, strategy enablement, and strategy execution, MP3 significantly enhances new demand creation performance over the traditional best-effort partner sales process. The MP3-Process element of our production line process takes inputs and turns them into predictable outputs, new pipeline!

■ **Performance**- Every production line requires system controls to identify constraints that are impacting productivity. MP3 offers an all-encompassing performance management framework. Our performance management framework establishes a novel suite of metrics specifically designed to capture and assess the execution of seller prospecting activity. Furthermore, MP3 introduces an innovative new ChannelOps math equation, crucial for managing our structured performance revenue creation process. The MP3 process shifts performance management to the individual partner sellers and target account engagement level. By doing so, we provide a level of actionable data and insights that are currently unparalleled, offering a granular view of performance that enhances decision-making and strategy refinement.

Figure 8.

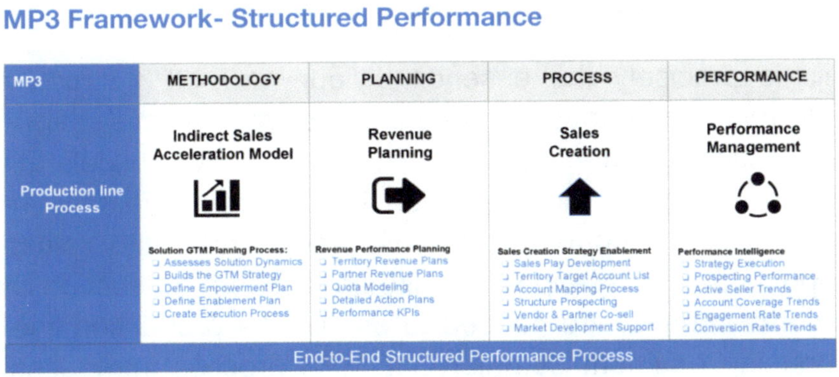

MP3 Framework- Structured Performance

MP3	METHODOLOGY	PLANNING	PROCESS	PERFORMANCE
	Indirect Sales Acceleration Model	**Revenue Planning**	**Sales Creation**	**Performance Management**
Production line Process				
	Solution GTM Planning Process: ❑ Assesses Solution Dynamics ❑ Builds the GTM Strategy ❑ Define Empowerment Plan ❑ Define Enablement Plan ❑ Create Execution Process	**Revenue Performance Planning** ❑ Territory Revenue Plans ❑ Partner Revenue Plans ❑ Quota Modeling ❑ Detailed Action Plans ❑ Performance KPIs	**Sales Creation Strategy Enablement** ❑ Sales Play Development ❑ Territory Target Account List ❑ Account Mapping Process ❑ Structure Prospecting ❑ Vendor & Partner Co-sell ❑ Market Development Support	**Performance Intelligence** ❑ Strategy Execution ❑ Prospecting Performance ❑ Active Seller Trends ❑ Account Coverage Trends ❑ Engagement Rate Trends ❑ Conversion Rates Trends
	End-to-End Structured Performance Process			

The MP3 Methodology represents a transformative data-driven structured performance partnering model crafted to significantly accelerate revenue growth. It serves as a foundational framework for companies aiming to harness the power of data-driven strategies and structured partnering processes to realize exponential growth. MP3 is modular, allowing companies to adopt individual elements or gradually phase in the entire process over time. Although the process is comprehensive, Channel Force has made it quite simple to adopt and deploy.

MP3 Is a Revenue Production Line Process

Now that we have introduced our framework, I want you to imagine your partner ecosystem sales process as a production line, a system carefully designed not to produce gadgets or widgets, but new sales. In every factory, raw materials are fed to the production line, processed through various stages, and emerge as finished products. Modern production lines monitor productivity, efficiency, and output, employing sophisticated control systems to identify and swiftly correct issues along the assembly line. Now, envision transforming the partner ecosystem sales process into such a production line, applying the same level of rigor and quality control mechanisms typical of a factory setting.

This is precisely the essence of our new MP3 structured performance methodology. In our model, the raw materials are the "active partner sellers." The MP3 sales acceleration process serves as the production line, where active seller and target account inputs are skillfully transformed into valuable outputs: "new sales pipeline." Like any modern production line, systems controls are needed to ensure the production line is producing optimum outputs. Our MP3 process introduces a new ChannelOps math equation and dashboard used to manage the production line process. MP3 effectively turns the partner ecosystem into a highly efficient sales engine. A system that churns out new opportunities when revenue leaders manage inputs (active sellers), equip the sales acceleration production line (sales play enablement, prospecting processes, account mapping, digital selling) and performance manage outputs (new leads), mirroring the precision and control of a traditional manufacturing operation.

A predictable revenue production line process with visibility and output control is what every CRO is looking for from their GTM channels. This is what MP3 and our toolsets are built to do! MP3 and our structured performance is the new leverage model making it easy, efficient and profitable for both vendors and partners. Figure 9 illustrates the components of our MP3 sales production line.

Figure 9.

MP3 Sales Production Line Process (Engine)

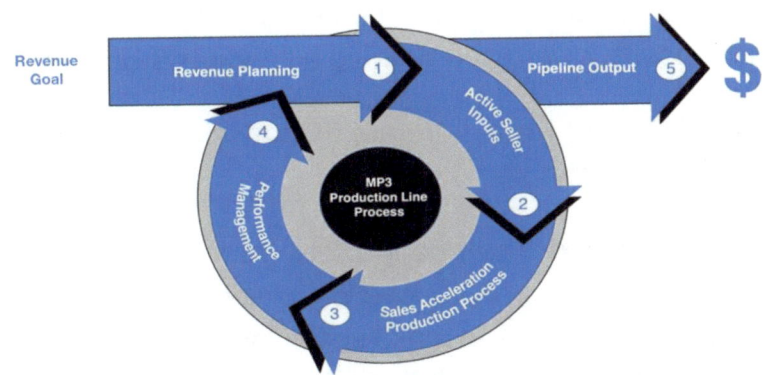

Summary

MP3 exemplifies the power of a data-driven structured performance partnering model to create greater leverage and better results. The remainder of this book will guide you through utilizing the MP3 process to build partner-sourced revenue engines. It offers the critical principles, processes, and best practices necessary to help you develop a next-generation revenue performance production line from your partner ecosystem. However, like any innovation, success requires an openness to change and a willingness to embrace new approaches and technologies. My hope is to break the status quo approaches ingrained in the partnering community unlocking the true sale potential of our partner ecosystems. As we embark on this journey, we will next explore the key partner model innovations that companies must consider to cultivate a robust revenue system through their partner community.

Chapter Application

This chapter covered significant ground. Consider your leverage model: Are you relying on the outdated belief that incentives alone motivate behavior, or are you facilitating your partner sellers' ability to execute your sales strategy effectively? Reflect on your partner GTM strategy: Are you establishing structured performance that leads to predictable revenue results, or are you running a "partner & pray" model?

CROs and Partner Pros, here are the key elements I want you to take from this chapter:

- **Structured Performance Models:** Are required in today's partnering landscape. Focus on planning and enhancing partner performance to make selling and support easier and more profitable. This includes addressing account coverage gaps and equipping partners with necessary selling skills.

- **New Leverage Models:** Evaluate the effectiveness of your leverage model: Is it generating active sellers? Does your enablement model make it easy and efficient for partner sellers to create new pipeline? Developing new principles and improved leverage models is crucial. This includes creating incentives that motivate sellers throughout the sales cycle and integrating structured selling techniques with playbooks.

- **Data-Driven Structured Performance:** Data-driven structured performance will soon become the new norm! Revenue Leaders must start utilizing partnership data to identify opportunities, refine strategies, and manage performance. This transformation in our partnership approaches will lead to increased organizational agility and improved partner alignment.

By adopting the MP3 model, you can transform your partner sales into a highly efficient "sales production line," applying rigorous control mechanisms to ensure optimal outputs. Our approach promises to realign traditional partnering models with current market demands and technological advancements to produce a new system designed to address the challenges of the opportunistic fulfillment model targeting 2x revenue growth at ½ the cost.

MODEL INNOVATIONS REQUIRED

4

In the previous chapters, we set the stage for a new partner sales methodology that leverages data and structure to deliver partner-led growth at an accelerated pace. We introduce our structured approach to revenue creation known as MP3:

- **M**ethodology (Production Line Blueprint)

- **P**lanning Revenue Production (Inputs)

- **P**rocess (Sales Production Line Process)

- **P**erformance Management (Outputs)

In this chapter, we will explore five process innovations that are fundamental to a next-generation structured performance process. These innovations are crucial for shifting from opportunistic program-centric partnering models to structured performance models. Essentially, these process innovations serve as the driving force behind the MP3 revenue creation engine.

The Need For Process Innovation

The traditional approach to partnerships and program development relies on instinct, relationships, and ad-hoc strategies (the art of partnering) to create sales activity. While these methods yield results, they are ill-equipped to meet the demands of today's rapidly changing business landscape. Several factors underscore the urgency for innovation:

- **Performance:** Unstructured partnering approaches are inefficient and underperform impacting revenue growth, drive expense and lower ROI.

- **Market Dynamism:** Markets evolve at an unprecedented pace, with customer needs and preferences shifting rapidly. Vendors must adapt quickly to remain competitive and meet these evolving demands.

- **Data Abundance:** We now have access to a wealth of data that can inform strategic decisions and enable more precise targeting. Failing to leverage this data is a missed opportunity for growth.

- **Increased Competition:** The vendor ecosystem is more crowded than ever, with more solutions vying for customers' attention. To stand out and succeed, vendors must adopt a more strategic, data-driven approach leveraging partners to gain entry to economic buyers.

- **Customer-Centricity:** Today's buyers are more informed and selective. They expect personalized, value-driven interactions. A one-size-fits-all approach is no longer sufficient.

- **Efficiency and Accountability:** In an era where every investment is scrutinized, partner programs must deliver measurable results and a clear return on investment.

To personalize this a little more, many best-effort partner sales models struggle to deliver results and with poor role-based attribution, inevitably putting jobs at risk! With these challenges in mind, the need for innovation becomes evident. We must transition from relying solely on intuition to embracing structured methodologies that leverage data, streamline processes, and deliver performance. The MP3 framework represents the Channel Force answer to this call for change – a systematic approach that equips organizations with the tools and strategies needed to excel in the modern channel landscape.

Five Process Innovations

Let's explore five foundational process innovations that underpin our MP3 framework. These innovations are essential to transforming the traditional partnering model. Each innovation targets a fundamental problem the program-centric partnering model is trying to address. To overcome the challenges of revenue, relevance, and ROI, we need to innovate the model. This involves integrating new strategies and tactics to directly tackle the core problem of unstructured, opportunistic fulfillment channels.

One: Prioritize Active Sellers (Prospecting)

Problem: The priorities of the program-centric approach are too far removed from the demand creation process, resulting in a lack of actionable data to enhance prospecting performance. Moreover, the program-centric model leads to a significant strategy execution visibility gap. Revenue leaders are forced to rely on partner-level data to make sales strategy decisions. These decisions are based on assumptions rather than prospecting data. This high-level focus on partner data complicates the resolution of performance and attribution issues, offering little in the way of managing sales activities with actionable intelligence. Traditional partner-level metrics only provide circumstantial evidence of a partner's effectiveness. For example, deal registration tells us "what and when" a partner achieves a result, but not "how" they achieve it. Additionally, the data, such as point-of-sale (POS) data, can take months to reconcile and is not very actionable. This results in channel management based on assumptions, with limited visibility into strategy execution and a focus that is too far removed from actual sales activities. This disconnect is a significant source of contention between partner organizations and sales teams, who often prioritize different aspects of the co-sell process leading to miscommunications and poor results.

Innovation: How can you create better partner-sourced sales performance? By refocusing your channel efforts on prospecting and actively measuring performance at partner seller and account levels. These changes not only make partnership data more relevant and immediate but also help to bridge the gap between partner and direct sales engagement, leading to a more cohesive and effective account-level sales strategy.

Shifting your measurement focus to individual partner seller prospecting activity enhances your influence in targeted accounts and reduces the costs associated with recruiting new partners. By capturing account-level prospecting activity, you gain the necessary visibility and influence to build better strategies that drive profitable and efficient revenue growth. This strategic shift helps us quantify true partner performance and moves us away from having to increase the number of partners to generate new activity. Shifting to active sellers allows you to measure the true production power and effectiveness of our partnerships. For more details, refer to Figure 10.

Shifting the focus to measuring strategy execution at the individual seller level offers several key benefits:

1. Activating an existing seller within a current partner organization is far more cost-effective than recruiting and onboarding new partners.

2. The 80/20 rule applies not just at the partner level but also among individual partner sales managers: 80% of partner sellers are dormant, reactively waiting to fulfill orders. There lies a significant opportunity to transform these sellers into proactive, sales-generators.

3. The time-to-value is considerably shorter with active sellers; you can organize, educate, and equip sellers to execute a selling strategy in just days, as opposed to the months it often takes to recruit and develop new partners.

The MP3 coverage model takes a more strategic approach by carefully planning prospecting activities with partner sales representatives mapping targeted engagements. This structured method improves how to organize, educate, equip, and measure partner sellers, moving away from traditional partnership models. By focusing more directly on prospecting performance, we introduce a new way of looking at GTM strategies, making them both data-driven and well-organized.

This evolution in partner-sourced sales execution creates a new approach to managing partners, continuously monitoring and optimizing performance with near real-time data and insights from prospecting activity. This ensures that partner sellers are not only well-informed and well-equipped but are also working within a system where their efforts are clearly and quantifiably attributed. This shift in performance management leads to a more strategic, responsive, and results-focused approach to partnerships, greatly improving the effectiveness and impact of partner-led GTM strategies.

Figure 10.

Active Sellers= Market Reach and Revenue Growth!

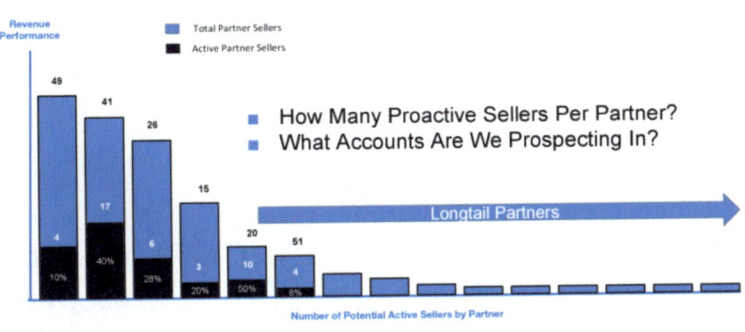

Additionally, focusing on measuring active sellers addresses the challenge of engaging longtail partners. By concentrating on activating individual sellers and providing them with a clear, step-by-step guide to generate new sales, you can methodically transform passive sellers into proactive prospectors, one at a time. Tracking the percentage of the partner's sales force that is active allows for the establishment of Key Performance Indicators (KPIs) to monitor and increase the number of new sellers each quarter. This approach not only boosts sales productivity but also enhances the overall performance of the partner ecosystem.

Note: Prioritizing active sellers gives us a new way to measure partner efficiency. By dividing by the number of active sellers prospecting, by the total number of salespeople a partner employs, provides us with a percentage of engaged sellers. This efficiency rating helps us develop KPIs and drive better partner engagement to improve efficiency rates. This is the true measure of a partner's commitment to your partnership.

Partner Sales Efficiency = Partner Active Sellers / Total Partner Sellers

Partner Efficiency provides revenue leaders with a metric to measure the production potential of the partnership and demonstrate active seller enablement trends, leading to partner revenue performance. KPIs can be established to effectively performance manage and monitor Partner Efficiency at the partner level.

Two: Packaged Prospecting

Problem: Given that the average partner seller has dozens of solutions in their portfolio, it's unrealistic to expect them to proactively promote a solution without a straightforward, easy-to-follow process. The absence of a structured prospecting process with a simple execution format represents a significant gap in the current partner sales model. While partner leaders cite account mapping and new account mapping platforms as the solution to their prospecting strategy, these efforts are sometimes challenged to yield results.

Typical account mapping issues stem from:

1. Inefficient account mapping processes.

2. Poor territory planning and co-sell alignment.

3. Insufficient resources to guide the prospecting effort.

4. Poor incentives to generate prospecting activity.

5. No structured measurement and accountability of prospecting activity.

6. Overly burdensome expectations placed on partner sellers.

To address these issues, it's crucial to adopt a structured prospecting process that simplifies and streamlines how partner sellers execute their outreach activities.

Innovation: MP3 Introduces the 4-3-2-1 method, a dynamic and structured partner-led prospecting process designed to complement and enhance the traditional account mapping approaches prevalent in partner sales today. See Figure 11. Partner sellers should be equipped with a process that addresses how to leverage their relationships and engage potential new accounts. To accomplish this, our innovative framework skillfully combines an organized account mapping process with a fully resourced prospecting strategy, streamlining lead development and maximizing efficiency. Recognizing the hectic schedules of sales professionals and the crucial importance of time management in achieving success, 4-3-2-1 is built on the principle of micro efficiency — breaking down tasks into smaller, manageable actions.

The 4-3-2-1 approach asks sales representatives to make a minimal yet impactful commitment of just ten minutes, three days a week for three weeks. This commitment is structured as follows:

- **4 Targets:** Identifying four key accounts or economic buyers to focus on. This step ensures that efforts are targeted and strategic.

- **3 Outreaches:** Sending out emails, invites, and social media outreaches every Tuesday. This regular, consistent communication built on a strategic messaging sequence helps cultivate engagement with potential leads.

- **2 Calls:** Making phone calls between the first and second email sequence every Thursday. These calls offer a more personal touch, increasing the chances of progressing to an initial engagement.

- **1 Alternative Approach:** Using one alternative approach, such as a referral or leveraging social media, to expand reach and network.

Figure 11.

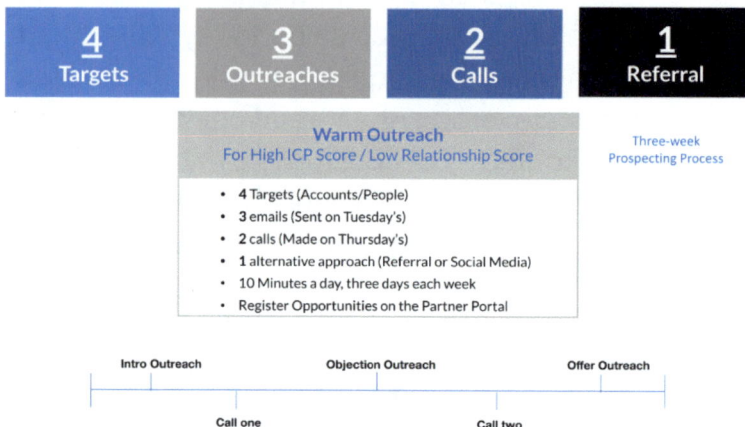

This methodical approach not only organizes the prospecting process but also ensures that sales professionals are consistently engaging with potential leads without overwhelming their schedules. The 4-3-2-1 promises to revitalize the prospecting process, making it more manageable and effective for busy sales professionals. The move to active sellers and the addition of a structured prospecting process allow us to turn partner sales into a mathematical equation. We can now define and manage the revenue production line process of the channel using a structured approach.

Three: New Channel Math Equation

Problem: Traditional channel analytics in many organizations tend to fall into two categories:

■ **Sales Metrics-** Historical sale achievement and forecast performance.

■ **Program Performance-** Program Performance- Centered around program compliance

While these metrics are crucial for assessing past results and potential future sales, they often fall short in providing deeper insights into the underlying factors driving these outcomes. Traditional methods are adept at presenting a snapshot of what has happened or what might happen, but they rarely delve into the reasons behind these trends. See Figure 12 for analytics evolution.

For instance, partner sales performance metrics are commonly used to gauge a partner's sales achievements over time, broken down by year, quarter, and product line. While this data can highlight positive or negative sales trends, it often leaves revenue leaders speculating about the causes behind these patterns. Without adequate context, such data can be misleading. A positive sales trend, for instance, might be interpreted as a sign of a partner's effective demand generation. However, if this trend is actually a result of the partner merely fulfilling the demand created by the vendor, or if it's influenced by a one-time event, then the interpretation of this data becomes flawed.

Figure 12.

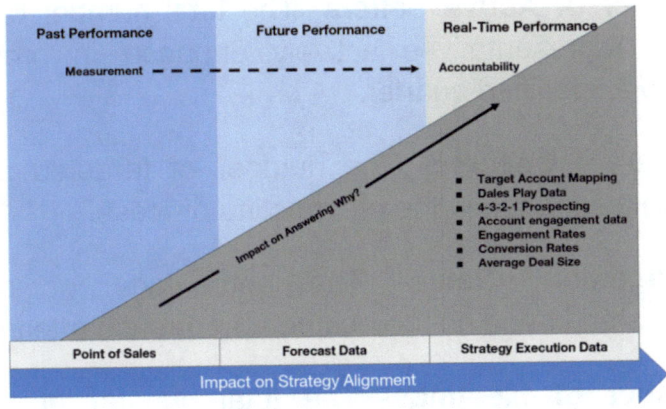

Analytics Evolution: Strategy Execution

Past Performance	Future Performance	Real-Time Performance
Measurement	→	Accountability

Impact on Answering Why?

- Target Account Mapping
- Dales Play Data
- 4-3-2-1 Prospecting
- Account engagement data
- Engagement Rates
- Conversion Rates
- Average Deal Size

Point of Sales	Forecast Data	Strategy Execution Data

Impact on Strategy Alignment

Another significant challenge with traditional program analytics is the manner of data capture. These analytics often rely on a combination of Point-of-Sale (POS) data and CRM systems, which track sales bookings and forecast data. While POS data offers a historical view of sales performance and forecasting provides insights into potential future sales, these metrics are more suited to opportunistic channel environments and fulfillment models. They are excellent for understanding what is happening or what has happened, but they don't effectively answer the critical questions of "How & Why?" This limitation can lead to a superficial understanding of channel performance, lacking the depth needed for strategic decision-making and long-term planning in channel management. Partner performance metrics, while important, fall short when it comes to sales performance management.

Innovation: This is where new ChannelOps math is required and a new view of channel performance. The traditional metrics are all partner-level metrics based on program-centric partnering models. MP3 process introduces a new ChannelOps math equation (See Figure 13) that measures the performance of your production line process to include:

- **Number of Active Sellers-** The total number of partner sales representatives actively engaged in prospecting within a specified quarter.

- **Accounts Covered-** The number of targeted accounts actively engaged in the prospecting process.

- **Engagement Rates-** The percentage of meetings generated based on the number of outreach attempts.

- **Number of Meetings-** The total number of meetings generated through prospecting efforts.

- **Conversion Rates-** The ratio of quoted opportunities as a percentage of meetings generated.

- **Average Deal Size-** The average size of all quoted opportunities.

The MP3 Model measures the sales production line process at the active seller and account level. In the program-centric partnering model, the measurement unit of production is the sales performance of the partner. In the MP3 Model, the measurement unit of production is active sellers. This downstream shift provides visibility and system controls that have been lacking. You can now draw a direct line from your strategy to partner seller activity and the sales results. This new ChannelOps math is a game-changer. It allows for a foundational shift in focus to manage partner-sourced production to deliver 2x revenue growth.

Figure 13.

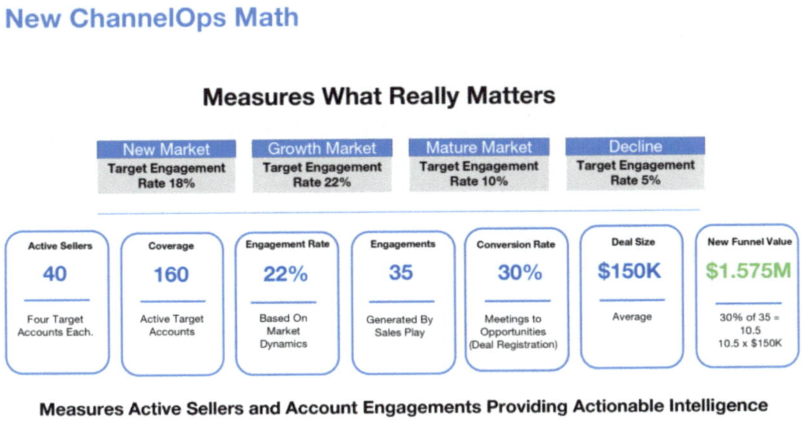

New ChannelOps Math

Measures What Really Matters

New Market	Growth Market	Mature Market	Decline
Target Engagement Rate 18%	Target Engagement Rate 22%	Target Engagement Rate 10%	Target Engagement Rate 5%

Active Sellers	Coverage	Engagement Rate	Engagements	Conversion Rate	Deal Size	New Funnel Value
40	160	22%	35	30%	$150K	$1.575M
Four Target Accounts Each.	Active Target Accounts	Based On Market Dynamics	Generated By Sales Play	Meetings to Opportunities (Deal Registration)	Average	30% of 35 = 10.5 10.5 x $150K

Measures Active Sellers and Account Engagements Providing Actionable Intelligence

Going back to our production line analogy, this new ChannelOps equation provides the system controls for the sales production line. Revenue leaders can manage the inputs and efficiencies of the production line to generate the desired outputs. In the MP3 process, the performance of the partner ecosystem is managed using this ChannelOps equation. By conducting a monthly trending analysis of each component within this equation at the sales play, partner, and PAM level, we perform a comprehensive health check on performance. This enables leaders to swiftly identify strengths and weaknesses, allowing for the implementation of strategies that either capitalize on opportunities or address and rectify any underperforming areas of our sales production line.

Standardizing on this new ChannelOps math equation demonstrates the power of a data-driven approach. ChannelOps math allows leaders to identify strengths, weaknesses, opportunities, and threats. We can now plan revenue growth and define the metrics needed to increase revenue at the ecosystem, partner, and channel account manager (CAM) levels. For example, doubling the number of active sellers and accounts doubles your prospecting efforts and revenue if your engagement rates, conversion rates, average deal size, and close rates remain the same. This is the transformative power of refocusing the partner performance model on active sellers and prospecting activity with targeted accounts.

Imagine the possibilities: By focusing on increasing the number of active sellers and the accounts they cover; you can achieve exponential growth. This approach provides clarity and predictability, enabling you to set clear goals, measure progress, and make informed decisions based on trends for each element of the equation. In addition, the shift to active sellers and target account coverage lowers the cost of the channel and speeds up the time to market. Gone are the days when we had to bear the persistent costs of continuously recruiting and onboarding partners just to achieve results. The transition to "active sellers" shifts our attention to cultivating new sellers within our existing partnerships, expediting the time-to-revenue while significantly reducing expenses!

Note: Our new ChannelOps math equation can be effectively applied at the partner level, enabling precise estimates of predictable revenue and the determination of a partner's potential. For instance, if a partner employs 20 salespeople, you can calculate the sales potential of this partnership for a given solution by considering engagement rates, conversion rates, and average deal size. Utilizing a Revenue Potential Score, you can then assess the strength of the partnership by comparing the actual revenue performance to the calculated revenue potential. For example, using a partner with 20 sellers, you can calculate partner potential using the following mathematical formula:

- **Total Addressable Sellers:** 20

- **Active Seller Unit:** Defined as each partner seller prospects in 4 target accounts per quarter.

To calculate partner potential start by defining the potentail enagements per quarter using the following:

- Formula: Total Sellers x Average Account Engagements Per Quarter.
- Example: 20 sellers x 4 engagements = 80 potential engagements per quarter.

- **Average Engagement Rate**: 20%. To find the projected meetings per quarter:

- Formula: Potential Engagements Per Quarter x Average Engagement Rate.
- Example: 80 potential engagements x 20% = 16 projected meetings per quarter.

- **Conversion Rate:** 30%. To determine the projected quoted opportunities:

  - Formula: Projected Meetings x Conversion Rate.
  - Example: 16 meetings x 30% = 4.8 quoted opportunities.

- **Average Deal Size:** $100K. To calculate the quarterly partner potential:

  - Formula: Quoted Opportunities x Average Deal Size
  - Example: 4.8 opportunities x $100K = $480K quarterly potential funnel.

- **Yearly Partner Potential:** To estimate the annual partnership potential:

  - Formula: Number of Quarters x Quarterly Potential Funnel
  - Example: 4 quarters x $480K = $1.92M in partner potential.

This example highlights the selling potential within a partnership and enables the channel to begin assessing partner efficiency. Using efficiency formulas, you can focus on enhancing partner productivity and reducing costs. This is just one instance of the various metrics that can be captured and analyzed through the new ChannelOps math, providing crucial insights into the productivity and effectiveness of the partner ecosystem.

Four: Shift To Strategy Enablement

Problem: Another shortcoming of the typical partnering model is the insufficient emphasis on sales strategy enablement. While the average enablement approach tends to concentrate on ensuring partners comply with program requirements and on training them about product value and use cases, these components, though crucial, don't fully equip partner sellers on how to sell. Strategy execution enablement is often overlooked, yet it is the most critical element for generating new sales. This gap highlights the need for a more comprehensive enablement process that goes beyond basic product knowledge to include robust sales strategy execution training for partners sellers.

Innovation: Our MP3 process is designed to provide a detailed, step-by-step sales playbook that guides partner sellers through a holistic sales process. It offers essential training on identifying high-probability accounts, understanding client needs, discerning key customer buying motivations, and effectively delivering a winning value proposition. Unlike typical marketing materials, the MP3 sales plays act as a comprehensive guide, teaching partner sellers the intricacies of navigating the sales process for a solution from start to finish. This includes detailed strategies for overcoming common objections, positioning the solution accurately, expanding sales reach, and closing deals successfully.

As such, partner enablement within our MP3 framework shifts from ensuring an understanding of your products and services to a more robust and practical training on solution-specific selling skills learning how to execute sales plays flawlessly. MP3 sales plays break down each step of the sales process and buyers' journey into stages. This allows for the creation of a step-by-step recipe to guide the demand creation and sales development of the partner seller.

Figure 14.

Sample Sales Play Framework

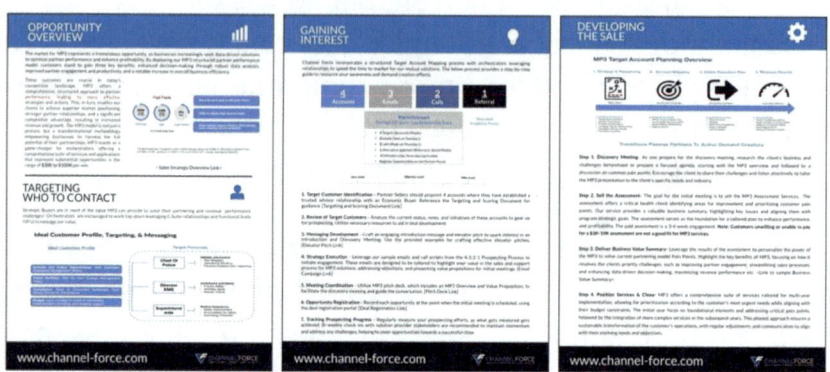

This transformation in enablement strategy ensures that partners are not just informed but are fully prepared to engage with clients to develop new sales. This focus on practical, actionable sales education is what sets our MP3 process apart, making it a vital tool in the arsenal of partner sellers. See the sample playbook example in Figure 14.

Five: Incorporate New Technologies

Problem: Partner-led growth is at the core of the MP3 strategy. A major hurdle for many partners is acquiring new customers. While MP3 offers a comprehensive process to mine partner sellers' relationships for new opportunities, there is still a need to help partners acquire new customers. In addition, there is an ongoing need to refine how partners deliver your solution value propositions, and educate, engage, and sell to clients. The answer is incorporating digital selling technology and artificial intelligence (AI) solutions into the partner GTM process. The demand for digital selling and AI solutions is growing exponentially, driven by a significant shift in buyer behavior; according to a Gartner study, 75% of today's buyers prefer not to interact with sales representatives (Gartner B2B Buying Report 2024). So, how can we enable partners to reach a wider audience and gather valuable customer insights? Incorporating digital selling technologies and AI into your channel's go-to-market model is crucial, as these tools can expand reach and enhance understanding of customer needs and behaviors.

Innovation: Implementing Digital Selling solutions has led to customers experiencing an 8x increase in engagements and a 50% reduction in Customer Acquisition Costs (CAC). The MP3 framework provides options to incorporate technologies like Splashmetrics Intelligent Buyer's Journey solution, which is designed to meet the needs of the modern consumer, and Ringdrop, an AI-powered prospecting tool to meet the needs of today's buyers.

Technologies like digital selling platforms provide a straightforward, interactive solution that guides customers through a customized buying process, enhancing their understanding and facilitating informed purchasing decisions. Modern digital selling platforms deliver tailored content based on the specific solution, use case, or user persona, creating a personalized and dynamic educational experience. Key elements of intelligent buyers' journeys include eBooks, case studies, assessments, ROI calculators, and demos. This approach not only effectively pinpoints customer challenges and emphasizes value propositions but also proactively addresses potential objections. Figure 15 outlines a typical workflow for integrating a digital selling platform into your partner GTM strategy.

Another promising technology is ai-driven prospecting. Companies such as Rigndrop.ai are advancing technology to facilitate AI-powered outreach and conversations that complement digital selling and account-based marketing, offering a multi-layered approach to pipeline creation and new account engagement. The MP3 methodology provides options to integrate these technologies and more into a structured partner GTM process to deliver exceptional results.

Figure 15.

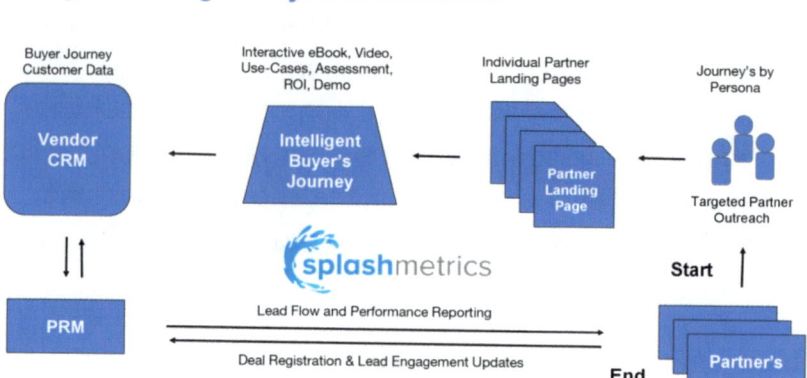

Chapter Application

It's crucial to comprehend the fundamental challenges associated with today's program-centric models and the innovations needed to build modern structured performance models. All structured performance models must apply new concepts to their go-to-market partnering strategies to solve the fundamental limitations of the common partnering model. Here are some key aspects CROs and Partner Pros should consider to applying the concepts outlined in this chapter:

One: Balance Program With Active Sellers

The essence of structured performance rests on transitioning from broad partnerships to directly organizing, educating, and equipping individual sellers. Partnerships primarily serve as conduits, granting access to sellers, accounts, and economic buyers. The real driver of sales performance is the activity level of these partner sellers. By equipping your sellers with a strong go-to-market strategy and measuring their performance through targeted account mapping, prospecting, and engagements, you can better assess the partnership's effectiveness.

Two: Standardize The Prospecting Process

Implement a dynamic and structured prospecting process, like the 4-3-2-1 method, to simplify and optimize the approach for partner sellers. Structured prospecting allows sales professionals to efficiently manage their time while ensuring regular engagement with potential leads. Regularly incorporating these prospecting activities into their routines can help turn passive sellers into active, proactive sales generators. 4-3-2-1 greatly boosts sales productivity. Additionally, this approach provides a consistent framework to measure seller productivity, ensuring clear metrics for success.

Three: Incorporate ChannelOps

Complement the traditional partner-level metrics with new ChannelOps math to better understand and influence partner performance. Track metrics like the number of active sellers, accounts covered, engagement rates, and conversion rates. This data-driven approach provides a clearer picture of channel performance, enabling targeted strategies that drive revenue growth and optimize partner engagement.

Four: Shift To Strategy Enablement

Focus on a comprehensive enablement process that goes beyond basic product knowledge. Implement detailed sales strategy training, which includes identifying high-probability accounts and delivering effective value propositions. This ensures that partners are not only informed but are also skilled in executing sales strategies that lead to successful outcomes.

Five: Incorporate Technology

Integrate technologies like digital selling platforms and AI prospecting to broaden your reach and improve customer engagement. Utilize tools that provide interactive and personalized experiences for customers, which can significantly reduce acquisition costs and increase engagement rates. These approaches also allow partners to better understand and respond to customer needs, enhancing the effectiveness of your go-to-market strategy.

By implementing these changes, you can revolutionize your partner sales process, enhancing its effectiveness, efficiency, and alignment with your company's revenue growth goals. These process innovations lay the groundwork for our MP3 process, enabling us to develop methodologies and tools that transform the traditional program-centric partnering model.

MP3-METHODOLOGY
(PRODUCTION LINE BLUEPRINT)

5

"Those who fail to plan, plan to fail." - Benjamin Franklin

One of the biggest gaps in today's partnering models is the lack of a defined partner sales creation methodology. In Chapter One, we highlighted the need for a structured sales creation process to complement today's common sales methodologies. MP3 is our answer to address the partner-sourced revenue sales methodology gap. MP3 provides a systematic sales creation process that defines:

1. The sales metrics needed to achieve a revenue goal.

2. The process to build territory and partner plans to resource the sales metrics.

3. A blueprint to customize a sales acceleration production line process

4. A partner performance intelligence process to measure productivity.

This structured performance process creates a comprehensive partner pipeline creation model, bridging partner sales and direct sales under a common co-sell framework. However, unlike the direct sales process, partner enablement is essential to drive solutions sales through the partner community, generating new opportunities that feed our co-sell process. We need a GTM planning methodology to develop marketing, partner strategy enablement, and sales execution plans.

Production Line Planning Process

This chapter introduces the MP3 Production Line Planning Process and outlines a set of best practices for planning your partner sales prospecting process. Each of the previous chapters have been foundational for building your knowledge of the issues we are addressing and the innovations we are applying to develop a new model. Now we will begin constructing the building blocks of our revenue engine starting with a foundational solution-based go-to-market planning methodology.

Indirect Sales Acceleration Model (ISAM)

At the heart of any effective go-to-market strategy lies planning. MP3 uses a comprehensive framework. The Indirect Sales Acceleration Model (ISAM), depicted in Figure 16, emphasizes a data-driven approach to developing solution-based GTM strategies.

Note: The ISAM methodology is detailed in the book "Channel Force." The following is a succinct overview of the model. For readers seeking a deeper understanding of the ISAM process Channel Force is available on Ingramspark and Amazon.

In addition, to clarify the distinction between ISAM and MP3: MP3 is the overall partner sales methodology that outlines the elements, processes, and frameworks for our partner-sourced sales methodology. ISAM is a subset of MP3 representing a five-phase solution planning process. The ISAM process serves as the blueprint to construct the sales acceleration plans for the MP3 production line process. To use an analogy, MP3 is the factory that produces the sales pipeline, while ISAM is the planning process that customizes the production line in the factory to optimize results.

Figure 16.

For those of you familiar with networking, you know the Open Systems Interconnect (OSI) model from the 1990s. The OSI model standardized the functions of a computing system into seven distinct layers: Physical, Data Link, Network, Transport, Session, Presentation, and Application. Each layer serves a specific function, building off the previous layer to facilitate communication and interoperability. Think of the ISAM model as the OSI model for Solution GTM Planning. The ISAM model creates a standard solution GTM planning model, starting with assessment and building through a process to an execution plan. The ISAM process consists of five stages defined as:

- **Assessment (Opportunity)**—Identifies a market need and assesses the market opportunity. This process answers the vital question, "Is this worth attacking?"

- **Strategy (Position)**—Maps out the solution sales strategy that will enable partners to create high-probability at-bats.

- **Empowerment (Awareness)**—Describes how to leverage partners to create new demand for a solution via indirect sales channels.

64

- **Enablement (Skills)**—Trains and equips partners to identify, qualify, position, develop, and close new sales.

- **Execution (Actions)**— Aligns the sales strategy to the target market, adding coverage, measurement and accountability.

As you think about building your solutions GTM plans, ISAM is a great way to assess your solutions market opportunity and build your marketing, partner enablement, and execution plans. All partner sales plans must address these elements to maximize results. The following is a condensed best practice version of the model.

Note: This chapter delves into the technical aspects of solution strength, market opportunity, and solution empowerment. The chapter introduces several new concepts and innovative approaches, such as strategy profiling, to effectively leverage data in the planning process. Effective planning must consider every factor that influences a solution's partner sales performance, ensuring a plan for each stage of a solution's sales journey. Please remember this is a high-level overview of the methodology.

ISAM Planning Elements And Considerations

Let's walk through each element of the ISAM model. Here are some best practices I teach companies to develop winning solution GTM strategies starting with the first stage of the ISAM Model "Assessment."

One: Assess The Opportunity

To develop a comprehensive go-to-market plan companies should evaluate four crucial elements that will influence the success or failure of a solution when sold through partnerships:

- **Solution Strength:** Your solution's ability to meet a market need and capture market share.

- **Market Opportunity:** The dynamics of the market that will influence your growth rates.

- **Partner Impact:** The capability of your partners to effectively market and sell your solutions.

- **Partner Rewards:** The effectiveness of your incentives to encourage proactive sales behaviors.

The interplay of these four elements will dictate the sales success of your solution when sold through partner ecosystems. The MP3 ISAM process assesses each element, assigning a level of strength to guide the development of targeted strategies.

Channel Force utilizes an assessment calculator that employs surveys and formulas to evaluate each of these four elements. However, for the purposes of this chapter, we will concentrate primarily on assessing solution strength. Here's why:

One of the quickest ways to undermine credibility with your partner community is by not fully understanding the market strength and potential of your solutions. Although companies often market their products as industry leaders with unique value propositions, it's essential for partners to possess positioning strategies and growth plans that reflect the actual merits of the solutions they are expected to sell.

How To Determine Your Solution Strength

Solution strength is determined by evaluating three elements:

- **Market Need** - Does your solution address a high-priority need that the market is actively seeking solutions for?

66

Options: Yes, Maybe, No.

- **Solution Fit** - Does your solution adequately meet the general requirements of the market need? Options: Yes, Maybe, No.

- **Competitive Strength** - How effectively does your solution compete against the top three competitors addressing the market need? Options:

  o My solution wins most of the time.

  o My solution wins about 50% of the time.

  o My solution loses most of the time.

Score your solution using the following points: Yes:10 Points, Maybe: 5 Points, No: 0 Points. Sum the scores from each category to determine the overall strength of your solution:

- A total score of 30 points indicates a Strong Solution.

- A score of 25 points is considered Favorable.

- A score of 20 points suggests a Competitive Solution.

- A score of 15 points or less signifies Low Strength.

Solution Strength and Market Opportunity are crucial factors that all partner sellers consider to decide whether to invest in selling your solutions. Nonetheless, the mandate from your company is to generate sales, regardless of your solution's strength. Understanding your solution's strength enables you to develop and adopt positioning and growth strategies that maximize sales while maintaining credibility with your partners. Solution Strength becomes the basis for building a GTM plan. Figure 17 presents four levels of solution strength, along with the corresponding positioning and growth strategies I recommend when advising clients.

Figure 17.

Assessing Solution Strength, Market Opportunity, Partner Impact, and Partner Compensation is foundational for a good GTM planning process. Understanding the strength of each of these elements sets the stage for the subsequent strategy development. The MP3 ISAM assessments ensure that every strategic decision is informed by data-driven insights, paving the way for effective planning.

Call to Action: Assess your solution strength, market opportunity, partner impact and partner incentives. Know how well you compete in each category. This will help you develop strategies to maximize your strengths and minimize your weaknesses.

Two: Solution Positioning Strategies

The second phase of the ISAM planning process involves taking assessment data to optimize your solutions positioning strategy. Having assessed a solution's strength, market opportunity, and partnership dynamics, companies now need to craft strategies that capitalize on strengths and mitigate weaknesses. The Sales Strategy phase leverages scores from each assessment to assign tailored strategies to each of the four assessment elements.

Upon completing the ISAM assessment and strategy phases, a strategy profile is created, as illustrated in Figure 18. This profile functions similarly to a Myers-Briggs personality test, outlining the strengths and corresponding strategies to maximize the sales potential of a solution. These strategy profiles clearly delineate a solution's strengths and weaknesses, enabling companies to strategically plan their approach to the market.

Defining Your Positioning & Growth Strategies

Strategy profiles address the need for detailed positioning and growth strategies in the partner sales enablement process. Strategy profiles:

■ Help determine how to effectively position a solution with the target market.

■ Identifies specific needs the solution addresses better than the competition.

■ Helps recognize opportunities to target aging install base solutions for replacement. Deciding which specific use cases or verticals to focus on to build sales plays are all critical considerations that can help target opportunities with the partners to mine their customer base. Targeting decisions should be guided by data-driven planning and fundamentally depend on the assessed market strength of your solution. Understanding these elements is crucial in shaping how to collaborate with partners to execute your solution sales strategy.

Solution Strength Strategy Alignment Example

Let's use 'Solution Strength' as an example, here's how specific positioning strategies are tailored for each identified level of strength:

- **Strong Solutions:** Emphasize challenging the market to find superior value, leveraging your solution's value proposition to capture and expand market share.

- **Favorable Solutions:** Focus on niche market segments where your solution has a distinct advantage, whether it be a specific feature, use case, or industry vertical.

- **Competitive Solutions:** Enhance your offering by pairing it with existing products to create a combined value proposition that surpasses what each can offer independently.

- **Weak Solutions:** Position your solution as a market disruptor by setting a lower price point. This strategy not only introduces a new floor price but also aims to erode the margins of competitors. Additionally, the strategy includes plans to capture new customers and implement effective upselling and cross-selling tactics to deliver stronger returns on investment.

In the ISAM planning process, each element—solution strength, market opportunity, partner impact, and partner compensation—is assigned a specific level of strength, with a corresponding strategy based on the identified strength. This enables the creation of a customized sales strategy tailored to each element. This framework enables companies to develop a flexible go-to-market strategy to develop their solution empowerment strategy.

Figure 18.

Sample Strategy Profile

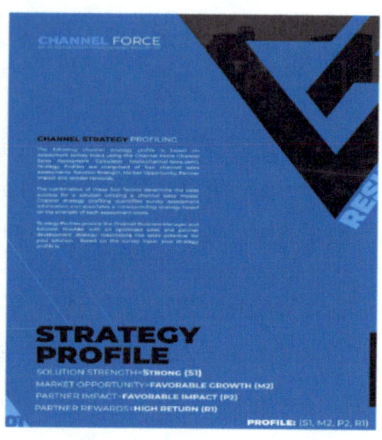

Call to Action: Channel Force offers a no-cost online calculator at www.channel-force.com that assesses Solution Strength, Market Opportunity, Partner Impact, and Partner Rewards. Completed each assessment, write down your strength for each element, and send an email to info@channel-force.com to receive your corresponding Strategy Profile.

Three: Solution Empowerment (Awareness)

Empowerment is the third phase of the ISAM model. This phase focuses on creating a comprehensive solution empowerment plan, encompassing marketing, market development, and sales strategies. It outlines how we will leverage partners to build awareness, convert that awareness into demand, and ultimately drive sales. The goal is to carefully plan how we will equip our partners with the necessary resources and tools to effectively generate demand. Empowerment uses strategy profiles to guide our planning process.

As you think about the most effective way to generate awareness for your solutions think about how you can provide a step-by-step empowerment plan for partners to follow. Virtually everything we use or consume in our daily lives comes with a set of instructions – from the cooking guidelines on packaged food, user manuals for technology products, to care labels on clothing. These instructions are crucial for guiding customers toward a successful use of the product. Surprisingly, in technology sales, such a clear, step-by-step guide to achieving the desired outcome – generating new sales – is often missing. However, imagine the transformative impact on revenue if partner sellers were provided with a comprehensive blueprint, a set of instructions designed to aid their efforts in creating new demand. This could significantly boost the performance of both underperforming passive partners and enhance the demand-creation capabilities of top active partners.

Revenue leaders frequently question: "What can we do differently to generate new revenue?" One promising avenue is the adoption of a formal empowerment process, equipping partners with the tools and guidance necessary to drive new sales. A well-structured blueprint clearly outlines the tactics that the partnering organization and the partner ecosystem should follow to generate new opportunities.

For many companies, the partner sales empowerment process is a compartmentalized, linear sequence. Initially, product marketing teams develop solution messaging, which is then utilized by sales and partner sales teams to build awareness and preference for a solution. Market development activities are either channeled through marketing departments or conducted alongside partners to cultivate the market within their customer base. Subsequently, leads are pursued by partner sellers to convert them into sales. Although this process can be effective, it doesn't necessarily foster an efficient system in which partners take full ownership of each aspect of demand creation. The MP3 Empowerment Model is built on the premise that partners should participate in every element of the demand creation process including marketing, market development and selling.

Empowerment Visualized As A Triangle

The MP3 empowerment process is visualized as a triangle. At the heart of our triangle is a solution-specific sales strategy developed through the ISAM process. Our solution sales strategies lay out a comprehensive plan for creating new sales, encompassing marketing tactics, market development initiatives, and sales approaches. Every aspect, from messaging and market development activities to sales plays, is carefully aligned to support the orchestration of the solution sales strategy.

The responsibility of the partnering team is to enable the partner ecosystem with the sales strategy, ensuring cohesive and effective execution. Partner Account Managers play a pivotal role in this process, organizing, educating, and equipping partners to execute this structured sales creation process. This approach not only creates a clear path for demand generation but also empowers partners with the knowledge and tools they need to succeed in today's competitive market.

Figure 19.

Partner Demand Creation Enablement Blueprint

A robust target account planning process fully integrates all elements of the MP3 demand creation process, setting the stage for effective and strategic partner engagement. By arming partners with a solution-specific selling strategy, coupled with well-defined sales plays, they gain a solid foundation for successful engagement. Defining target accounts is a critical part of this process, ensuring that partners focus their efforts on the most promising opportunities.

In addition to these strategic elements, creating compelling messaging is key to capturing and maintaining the interest of potential customers. This messaging is aligned by the sales stage to the entire buyer's journey for a solution, ensuring a seamless and persuasive narrative from initial contact through to deal closure.

Furthermore, resourcing active seller engagement across all stages of the buyer's journey is essential. This comprehensive support empowers partner sellers with the tools and resources to effectively engage with potential clients, address their specific needs, and guide them toward a positive buying decision.

Training and resourcing partners on how to develop and close new deals is the final piece of the puzzle. This training provides them with the necessary skills and knowledge to identify potential sales opportunities and to convert these opportunities into successful transactions.

By combining these elements – a tailored selling strategy, targeted account focus, compelling messaging, full-spectrum resourcing, and comprehensive training, proper incentives – you effectively provide partners with a blueprint for successful demand creation.

The ISAM model employs this demand creation blueprint to

develop empowerment plans that engage partner sellers at each stage of the pyramid. Additionally, these empowerment plans outline the resources required to execute each element of the pyramid effectively. As mentioned, the book Channel Force defines the empowerment process in detail.

Call to Action: Work with your marketing teams and build your partner enablement plan and collateral based on your solution positioning and market development strategies. Define what you expect of your partners in each element of the demand creation pyramid. Build your marketing plans and resource the actions.

Four: Strategy Enablement (Skills Development)

The MP3 ISAM Enablement process builds on the assessments, strategies, and empowerment phases, teaching partner sellers how to position and sell solutions. The ISAM partner strategy enablement process goes beyond traditional product-centric enablement approaches. By integrating strategy enablement, ISAM enhances how partners engage with and sell solutions. This ensures your partners are not only knowledgeable about the products but also skilled in executing effective sales strategies. This process involves a detailed understanding of the marketplace, the specific challenges partners face, and the competitive dynamics that influence sales outcomes. The goal is to equip partners not just with product facts but with a robust process and toolkit for engaging customers, understanding their needs, and delivering solutions aligned with strategic business goals. Here is the enablement process I teach:

Program Basics-> Product Knowledge-> Sales Process-> Skills-> Selling Strategy

Your enablement training should include all of the following elements:

- **Incentive Program Overview:** Outlines the benefits for the seller, defining the partner program basics and expected compensation for an average deal.

- **Product Knowledge:** Provides a solution overview and value proposition training, defining what we do (use cases), why we do it (outcomes), and what makes us special (unique benefits).

- **Sales Process Training:** Defines how to identify high-probability accounts (ideal customer profiles), the buyer's journey stages, the average sales cycle, and the level of effort to close a sale.

- **Skills Training:** Details best practices for positioning the solution by persona, identifying common objections and strategies to overcome them, and defining buying motivations by persona, along with best practices.

- **Selling Strategy:** Defines the call to action, specifying what you want the seller to do (identify four accounts), when you want them to do it (this month), and how you want it done (execute sales play steps). Remember to reiterate the benefits for the seller in executing the sales strategy.

The MP3 planning process defines the training needed at each stage. Additionally, packaging the enablement in the form of sales play training allows sellers to learn as they progress. This just-in-time sales training approach teaches sellers at each step in the sales process as they work through the sales play. Just-in-time training makes learning efficient and relevant for each sales stage. It is also less time-consuming. The result of your strategy enablement training should produce confident active sellers!

Note: Sales plays are essential tools for motivating partner sellers to prioritize your solution. When properly enabled, sales plays transform passive salespeople into active sellers. I cannot stress enough the importance of developing high-quality sales plays and prioritizing strategy enablement. Sales plays and strategy enablement are fundamental to building your production line process. See Figure 20 for a sales play example.

Figure 20.

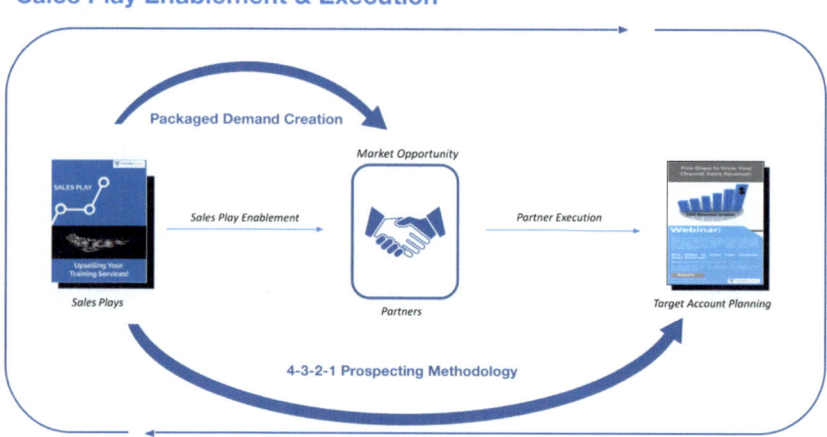

Finally, strategy enablement involves teaching a structured coverage model and target account planning process. The "Call to Action" to end every enablement session is a formal account mapping exercise. The ISAM process leverages Strategy Profiles and Empowerment Planning to create impactful, solution-specific enablement.

Call to Action: Define your enablement plan by starting from the customer pain point and working backward to your solution. It's easy to forget that sellers are primarily focused on making money, not our solutions. The goal of your enablement is to create highly productive active sellers. Ensure you support the strategy by highlighting what's in it for the seller, not just the product. A good strategy enablement plan produces active sellers.

Five: Sales Execution (Actions)

The final planning phase of the ISAM model is the execution stage. What do we want our partner sellers to do to create demand? The execution plan integrates the assessment, strategy, empowerment, and enablement processes into a structured coverage, Target account planning, and co-sell process to deliver results. Your execution plans should be structured enough for every partner to follow the same process, yet flexible enough to allow partners to define their unique value.

The execution stage of the ISAM framework incorporates a territory coverage and target account planning process. This phase furnishes an actionable plan at the seller level, synthesizing the entire planning process to pinpoint high-probability accounts. It empowers sellers to proactively engage with clients, facilitating an initial step in the sales process that sets the stage for potential transactions. This strategic approach ensures that every move is calculated to optimize engagement and maximize the chances of successful outcomes.

Figure 21.

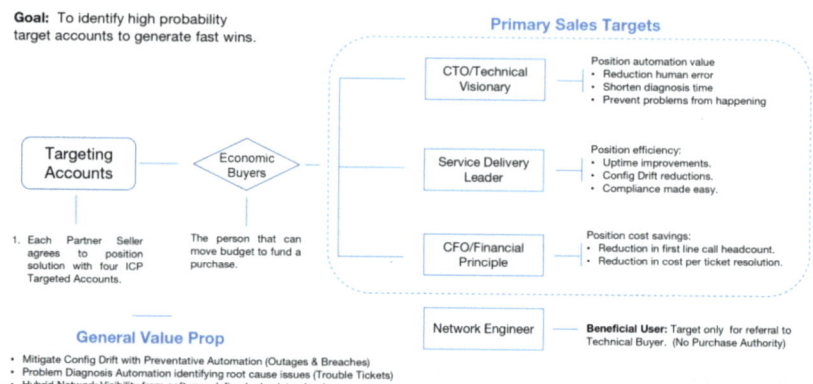

Sample Targeting & Messaging Example

As we move forward through subsequent Chapters, we cover execution planning in detail.

Conculsion

The goal of this chapter was to lay the foundation for our planning methodology, which is designed to develop effective, solution-based GTM plays that enhance your production line process. The ISAM planning process coordinates all organizations involved in solution planning and sales execution under a unified framework to produce successful sales GTM plans.

Chapter Application

Consider your solution sales planning process. Are you evaluating solution strength, market opportunity, partner impact, and incentive effectiveness in your planning process? Are you developing your marketing, sales enablement, and strategy execution plans based on the unique capabilities of your solution? If not, you're not alone!

A significant challenge plaguing many channels is the lack of a formalized solution planning process that tailors go-to-market strategies to capitalize on the unique strengths of their solutions and partner ecosystems. The Indirect Sales Acceleration Model offers a comprehensive framework designed to develop impactful GTM strategies. By addressing this gap in today's channel planning process, ISAM enables a more structured approach, enhancing the effectiveness of your partnerships and aligning strategies with the dynamic needs of modern sales environments. Here are some best practices:

One: While the process may seem daunting, and for many companies the elements of our ISAM model span multiple departments, one best practice is to align cross-functional teams using the ISAM model. This approach helps unify the organization under a common vision for solution planning.

Two: Develop your own strategy profiles for your solutions. Use data to define your solution's strengths, market opportunities, partner impact, and incentive strength. Build strategies for each element and level of strength. This forward-thinking approach will help you maximize the sales potential of your solutions when sold through the channel. On a side note, Channel Force can assist with this process.

Three: Be sure to consider how to utilize your partners in all three aspects of the demand creation process. Define how partners can market your solutions, develop the market, and drive sales. The enablement pyramid is an excellent visual tool to guide your empowerment and enablement plans. Partners that proactively market, develop the market and sell, take ownership of the sales creation process and deliver better results!

Four: Finally, use data to develop sales plays. Sales plays simplify the enablement and sales development process for sellers. A good sales play transitions passive partner sales reps. into active sellers when enabled and resourced properly!

Now that we have covered production line planning, Let's address revenue planning!

MP3 PLANNING REVENUE PERFORMANCE (INPUTS)

6

Frederick Taylor, Karol Adamiecki, and Henry Gantt were pivotal figures in revolutionizing the efficiency of modern production lines. Frederick Taylor, often regarded as the father of scientific management, introduced methods to optimize human labor. Frederick used time and motion studies, advocating for the scientific training of workers and the division of labor. This approach greatly enhanced productivity by identifying the best methods for performing specific tasks.

Karol Adamiecki developed the Harmonogram, an early form of the Gantt chart, which visually represented schedules in production processes. This tool was instrumental in planning and maintaining operations within a factory. Henry Gantt, whose name is immortalized in the Gantt chart, expanded on Adamiecki's concepts to provide a more comprehensive tool for scheduling and monitoring project tasks. Gantt's charts were crucial during World War I, helping to manage the production and logistics of American armaments. Together, these pioneers laid the groundwork for modern project management and operational efficiency in production environments, significantly influencing how industries manage both time and resources to maximize output. Can we apply production line management and efficiency principles to partner sales operations through ChannelOps?

The RevOps Revolution

Revenue operations (RevOps) has been at the cutting edge of sales process innovation for the past decade, transforming sales methodology and planning into a science. Companies now leverage data to craft their GTM strategies and achieve better results. Yet, the partnering model remains the final segment of the sales puzzle to embrace a data-driven performance model, primarily due to a lack of process innovation. As discussed, the partner GTM process needs to evolve to create and measure proactive sellers, focusing on account-level prospecting. This shift is crucial for RevOps to develop a robust partner seller metrics model that goes beyond high-level partnership metrics to strategy execution metrics that provide actionable insights.

The MP3 methodology is designed to move the planning metrics downstream to the partner seller and account prospecting level to harness the transformative potential of partner sellers. By innovating the partnership sales acceleration GTM process, we are bringing ChannelOps to the forefront transitioning from the ad hoc "partner and pray" models to a structured, data-driven performance model. We are turning the partner sales model into a production line system. Our systematic approach streamlines operations, enhances predictability, and improves the effectiveness of the partnering organization to achieve the sales target. Using our production line metaphor, The MP3 Revenue Planning Phase clearly defines the inputs to our partner sales creation system to predict and control pipeline output.

This chapter introduces a new approach to revenue planning aimed at empowering channel teams and partners with visibility to the sales metrics required to surpass their revenue goals. By outlining required sales metrics, we will help partner organizations optimize their demand creation performance in a measurable and scalable way.

Channel Force has designed a ChannelOps process and toolkit that pinpoints the most crucial metrics for partner-sourced sales creation, devises a strategy to boost the number of active sellers, and implements performance management procedures to guarantee optimal efficiency in your channel operations.

In the sections that follow, I will delve into each component of the revenue planning process, providing you with practical insights to maximize your partner ecosystem's potential. Whether you're a vendor seeking to enhance your ecosystem strategy or a partner looking to optimize your sales approach, a data-driven methodology empowers you to take charge of your performance destiny and deliver on the promise of achieving 2x revenue growth.

Planning Metrics: The Power Of Planning

Partner sales is complex and success is measured by the achievement of revenue targets. Every vendor aspires to see their solutions sales consistently growing, while partners aim to maximize their return on investment. In pursuit of these shared objectives, revenue planning plays an important role, serving as the compass that guides vendors and sellers toward sales achievement. However, traditional channel planning has long relied on high-level partner plans and loose revenue targets, leaving much to be desired in terms of precision and predictability. In essence, territory and partner planning has been a "partner and pray" approach, where success was uncertain, and results were left to chance.

The traditional approach to channel planning leaned heavily on partner relationships and subjective estimations, lacking the robust data and sales metrics necessary for informed decision-making. This has led to a significant gap between aspirations and actual outcomes. We need a new approach—one rooted in data, metrics, and a carefully crafted roadmap to revenue achievement.

A New Approach: Data-Driven Planning

Imagine a world where every key aspect of your channel sales performance is planned, with critical metrics, activities, and timeframes defined to inch you closer to and eventually beyond your revenue target. This is the essence of data-driven revenue planning—a revolutionary approach that replaces ambiguity with precision and turns aspirations into actionable strategies. See Figure 22.

Figure 22.

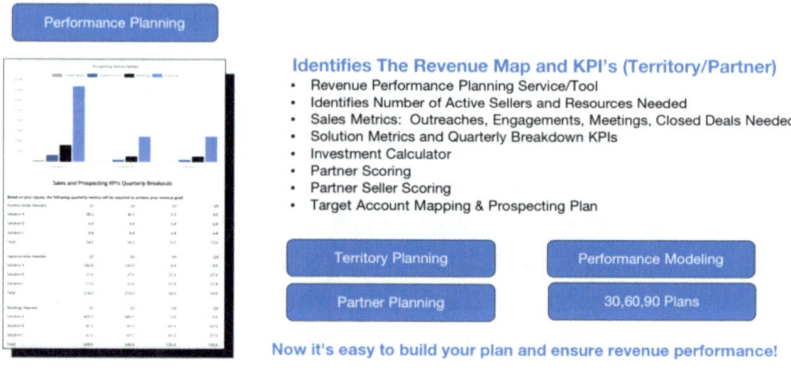

Data-Driven Performance Planning

Performance planning hinges on leveraging data to construct comprehensive revenue roadmap plans that define the exact metrics needed for success, who is responsible for each aspect, when it should be executed, and how it will be achieved. The process breaks down into five essential steps:

- **Define the Data Inputs:** The cornerstone of any data-driven strategy is the data itself. To ensure the success of your channel sales territory, it's crucial to identify the essential data inputs. These include your revenue goals, and metrics for your solution set such as average deal size, monthly sales cycles, engagement rates, and close rates.

Additionally, methodology metrics are vital, covering aspects like target account planning metrics, the number of active sellers per partner, and more. These inputs form the basis for your revenue roadmap plan.

- **Use ChannelOps Tools to Calculate Inputs:** Utilizing new tools like our Planning IQ (Channel Force Revenue Planning Software) allows companies to organize, and analyze data inputs. These tools will become the engines driving your revenue roadmap, providing insights that were previously hidden in the chaotic sea of information. Our new ChannelOps tools define the metrics and timeframes that need to be achieved by territory and partner to ensure the revenue goal is met.

- **Output the Metrics and Timeframe KPIs:** With data outputs in hand, determine the key performance indicators (KPIs) and the timeframe for achieving them. These metrics will serve as the guiding star to build the execution plan for your revenue journey.

- **Take Each Metric and Define Who, When, How:** Assign ownership of each metric to specific individuals, accounts and partners. Define when each metric should be measured and how it will be achieved. This clarity ensures accountability and execution excellence. For example, if the revenue roadmap report requires forty active sellers to generate the revenue, build your execution plan defining who each active seller will be.

- **Build a Detailed Revenue Plan:** Incorporate all the elements of your plan into a comprehensive revenue roadmap. This should include partner contributions, seller responsibilities, and the target accounts that will drive revenue.

Territory Revenue Planning Starts With Data

Data-driven territory and partner planning leverages various data inputs to create a comprehensive and effective plan. Our method ensures that every aspect of the territory and channel management is optimized for maximum efficiency and profitability. Like any data-driven model, the quality of the inputs will determine the accuracy of the output. As we start our planning process the model requires some key data points to include:

- **A Revenue Target:** The primary financial goal for the territory or partner over a specific period.

- **Ecosystem Management Metrics:** This encompasses the number of active sellers each Channel Account Manager oversees per quarter, providing insight into the strategy execution and prospecting activity of the sales force.

- **Average Number of Active Sellers per Partner:** A metric that gauges the engagement and capacity of each partner in the sales process.

- **Solution Sales Metrics:** Average deal size and the length of a solution sales cycle.

- **Targeted Engagement Rates:** Defines the number of meetings generated as a percentage of Target Account Mapping engagements.

- **Conversion Rates:** The percentage of first meetings that progress to a quoted opportunity, indicating the effectiveness of sales strategies and tactics.

- **Close Rates:** The ratio of successful sales to the number of sales opportunities, reflecting the efficiency of the sales process.

■ **Average Deal Size:** An average value of sales transactions, providing insight into the market's purchasing patterns and the value proposition of the offerings.

By analyzing these data inputs, we have built a data-driven planning tool that delivers a summary of critical metrics. This summary serves as the foundation for developing a robust territory plan. It highlights areas of strength and opportunities for improvement, guiding decisions on resource allocation, sales strategy, and partner management. This data-centric approach ensures that territory and partner plans are not only aligned with business objectives but also responsive to the dynamics of the market and customer needs. See the Output Territory Summary Sample in Figure 23.

Figure 23.

The Summary Output Report in Figure 23, is a sample report from the Channel Force Planning IQ Tool and exemplifies the capabilities of data-driven planning. This summary report is one of 12 reports available through the Planning IQ tool and offers a detailed overview of the essential metrics needed to achieve the specified territory revenue goal.

Revenue planning tools equip leaders to effectively model revenue strategies, allowing them to evaluate the feasibility of each team member's revenue goal and the effort required to achieve the goal. Revenue planning is an evolution to the partnering process that goes beyond simply assigning quotas allowing leaders to include a detailed, pre-scripted metrics summary to guide the Channel Manager in their territory planning process. Revenue Roadmap Reports serve as a foundational baseline to build a tailored revenue plan for the territory, ensuring that the strategy is not only goal-oriented but also rooted in realistic, data-driven expectations. Data enriches the strategic planning process, providing leaders with a clearer route to achieving their objectives and ensuring team alignment with a comprehensive, actionable plan.

Let's explore how data-driven planning revolutionizes revenue performance. Using the data from Figure 22, the summary output indicates a need for 15 partners, 218 Seller Units (one seller executing 4-3-2-1), and 653 outreaches to economic buyers to meet the goals. With these metrics, we can construct a Territory Plan starting with the number of partners needed to reach the revenue targets.

- **Number of Partners Needed:** The determination of the number of partners needed is a crucial aspect of strategic planning, especially when it comes to achieving set revenue goals. This number is not arbitrary but rather a calculated estimate based on several key factors that influence a partner's potential contribution to the revenue target.

The planning process involves a thorough evaluation of partners, scoring them on various criteria such as their market reach (specifically, their access to the target market), the potential of active sellers they have (which indicates the capacity for driving sales), their competency in selling the specific solution (a measure of how well they understand and can effectively market the product), and the level of priority they are likely to give to prospecting for the solution (indicating their commitment and alignment with the business goals). A formal scoring process is employed to objectively assess these factors, leading to the identification of the top partners. See Partner Impact Scoring Process in Chapter 7.

For our specific plan, this rigorous evaluation process aims to pinpoint the 13 most suitable partners. These selected partners are expected to play a pivotal role in supporting and fulfilling the strategic objectives laid out in the revenue plan, each partner will contribute in a unique way to the overall goal based on their strengths and capabilities.

- **Active Sellers Needed:** The concept of "Active Sellers Needed" focuses on quantifying the number of individual sales representatives required from partner organizations. In our approach, we define an active seller in terms of 'units,' with one unit representing a seller's potential within a quarter. Since a year comprises four quarters, an active seller theoretically represents up to four units annually. However, this sales potential diminishes for sellers enabled later in the year, as they have fewer remaining quarters to actively engage in prospecting for our solutions. This unit-based system helps in determining the total number of seller production units we need to create throughout the year to achieve the number.

In our model, we are scoring potential sellers evaluating their alignment with our goals, capacity to drive sales, and overall potential as an active contributor. This detailed evaluation aims to identify the most suitable individuals who will be classified as active sellers, integral to achieving our annual objectives. This structured approach ensures that we not only align with the right partners but also engage with the most effective individual sellers within those partnerships. In our example, we defined the need for 197 Seller units. We can now start to name the individuals that we focus our efforts on to meet the metric.

- **Outreaches Needed:** The metric "Outreaches Needed" quantifies the necessary individual contacts with economic buyers to meet the revenue target. This number is closely tied to the range of personas being targeted, as different personas often necessitate outreach to varied accounts. Essentially, the more personas you aim to engage, the lower the number of accounts that must be included in your partner prospecting efforts.

The calculation of the required number of accounts is directly influenced by the diversity and quantity of these target personas. Once established, this figure translates into a specific outreach goal, which is then integrated into the individual plans of each partner. It sets a clear objective for the targeted account planning process, guiding the allocation and focus of outreach efforts.

This framework not only streamlines the outreach strategy but also facilitates a more organized approach to account identification. By working collaboratively with individual partner sellers, accounts can be methodically mapped and targeted, ensuring that outreach efforts are aligned with the defined personas and contributing effectively towards the overall revenue goal. This systematic approach ensures that every outreach is purposeful and strategically aligned with the overarching sales objectives.

Our data-driven territory planning process can produce up to twelve different reports breaking down the metrics by solution, quarter and revenue.

Partner Revenue Planning

While partner planning is a well-established practice in the channel, with a decades-long history of setting revenue goals, initiatives, MDF funding, co-marketing activities, and targeting specific accounts, traditional approaches have their limitations. Typically, these traditional plans excel in outlining broad objectives but often fall short in detailing the specific sales metrics, activities, and timelines necessary for achieving these revenue goals. Furthermore, a common shortfall of these conventional plans is their disconnection from the overarching vendor and solution sales strategies. This disconnect results in plans that are not only poorly integrated with the main sales strategy but also lack sufficient resources, methodology, and structured coverage.

This is where partner revenue roadmaps excel. Partner revenue planning addresses these gaps by integrating partner plans with the overall solution sales strategy. The MP3 process provides a comprehensive framework that includes not just goals and objectives but also a detailed breakdown of the methods and activities required to achieve them. This approach ensures that partner plans are not just a set of isolated objectives but are closely aligned with the vendor's strategy, well-resourced, and supported with a clear methodology, sales plays, and structured coverage. Revenue planning represents a significant evolution in partner planning, making plans more strategic, integrated, and effective.

Partner Planning Process

In the MP3 partner revenue planning process, revenue generation is accomplished through two primary methods: structured account mapping and market development. The MP3 partner planning process begins by setting a revenue goal for each priority partner, which is a smaller portion of the

Channel Account Manager's (CAM) broader territory goal. The revenue goal is split between target account mapping and traditional market development activities. By breaking down the revenue goal into distinct categories and incorporating information such as cost per lead, outbound and inbound revenue mix, and event-related revenues, we create a comprehensive framework for revenue planning.

Figure 24.

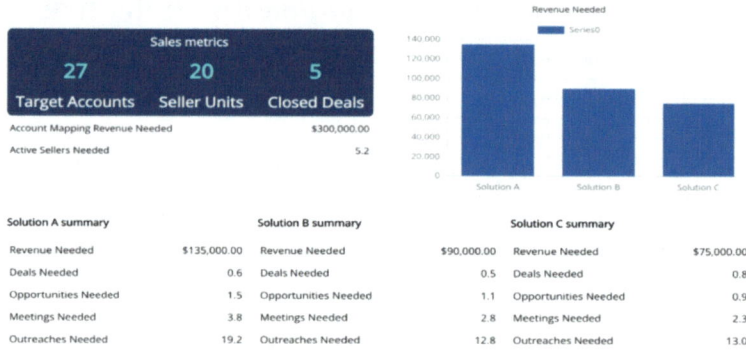

Partner Revenue Roadmap Account Mapping (Example)

Target Account Planning (Partner)

The target account mapping plan is based on a revenue target we are looking to achieve through leveraging account relationships. The MP3 ChannelOps inputs require the following data inputs to generate the partner revenue plan:

- **Revenue Target:** The financial goal set for the period.

- **Number of Personas Targeted:** The specific buyer or user personas that the sales efforts will focus on.

- **Solution Sales Metrics:** Average deal size, sales cycles, engagement rates, etc.

- **Market Development Metrics:** Engagement rates for campaigns, events and inbound lead generation.

- **MDF Price Per Lead:** The cost associated with generating leads through Market Development Funds (MDF).

These categories of inputs are essential for calculating the sales metrics needed to surpass the annual revenue goal. Figure 22 shows an example of a target account planning report generated using our Planning IQ software. Partner Account Managers collaborate with partners to set revenue goals and then work with ChannelOps to create detailed revenue roadmaps. Once these metrics are in place, Partner Account Managers and partners work together to develop comprehensive partner action plans tailored to these metrics.

Market Development Planning

This plan explicitly outlines the target account planning metrics – the specific accounts and strategies that the partner needs to focus on. It also includes the market development metrics, which detail the various market engagement and development activities required to not only meet but exceed the set revenue goals. This structured approach ensures that every aspect of the partner's role in achieving the revenue target is clearly defined and aligned with the overall sales strategy, providing a clear path to success. See the Market Development Metrics Example in Figure 25.

Figure 25.

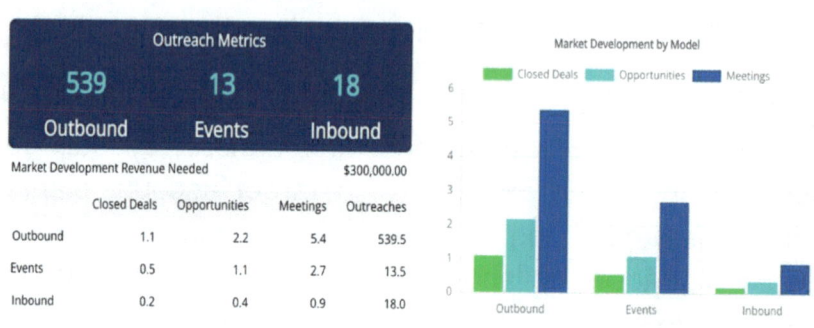

Partner Market Development Metrics (Example)

In addition to specifying the performance required for target account mapping, the partner revenue roadmap details the market development metrics and MDF investments necessary to surpass revenue targets. Market development activities include account-based marketing outreach, market development events, and enhancing online presence through digital selling tools like Splashmetrics intelligent buyer's journey solution. Our ChannelOps planning process determines the appropriate mix and metrics for both strategies.

MDF Planning

If we expect partners to commit time, money, and resources to generate new leads, it is crucial to have a formal Market Development Funds (MDF) planning process in place to support their investment efforts. Our revenue planning methodology includes a toolset that facilitates MDF planning, based on the cost per lead source. In our approach, we compensate partners for Partner Qualified Leads generated through our structured performance process. Figure 26 illustrates a sample MDF report that details the incentive budget and MDF allocations associated with the plan.

Figure 26.

Partner Market Development Funding Metrics (Example)

			MDF Policy		50%
Incentive budget Per Lead					$200
Incentive Policy					50%

	Opportunities	Average CPL	Total Cost	MDF Funding
Outbound	2.2	$1,000.00	$2,157.95	$1,078.98
Direct Engagement	1.1	$1,000.00	$1,078.98	$539.49
Inbound	0.4	$1,000.00	$359.66	$179.83
Total	3.6		$3,596.59	$1,798.30

The MP3 Partner Revenue Planning process establishes metrics for target account planning and market development sourced leads. Partner Revenue Roadmaps offer a framework for partners and CAMs to collaborate outlining resources, accounts, personnel, timeframes, funding, and activities to create a detailed, measurable, and actionable plan.

Chapter Application

Revenue Planning is an innovative concept and signifies a significant evolution in revenue operations to encompass ChannelOps. Change is a constant in all aspects of life, and although adapting can be challenging, considering the traditional partnering model - "We are the anomaly." Think about it, nearly everything we purchase, or use comes with instructions—from our clothing and appliances to our food— guiding us on how to use, set up, consume, support, or prepare the product. Similarly, the partnering model is now progressing towards the norm, with a systematic approach that enables us to construct detailed plans and instructions to optimize performance.

The MP3 Revenue Planning Process represents a significant evolution from the traditional 'partner and pray' approaches, offering a more strategic and data-driven methodology. Using our production line concept, companies can now precisely define inputs to the sales acceleration process necessary to not only achieve but also exceed their revenue goals. This clarity in metric definition allows for the creation of detailed action plans tailored to both territories and partners. These plans identify the key metrics and resources required for success – including the right people, targeted accounts, specific activities, and set timeframes. This comprehensive approach ensures a higher level of precision and alignment, moving away from reliance on chance and towards a more structured, accountable, and results-oriented strategy. The benefits of revenue planning are numerous:

- **Precision:** Replace guesswork with data-backed strategies, ensuring that every effort is focused on achieving measurable results.

- **Accountability:** Assign responsibilities for each metric, fostering a culture of ownership and accountability within your sales team and partner network.

- **Visibility:** Gain real-time visibility into your progress, allowing you to spot bottlenecks and opportunities early, and adjust your strategies accordingly.

- **Adaptability:** In a constantly evolving marketplace, the ability to adapt quickly is paramount. A well-defined revenue roadmap empowers you to pivot when needed.

- **Optimized Resource Allocation:** Efficiently allocate resources where they are needed most, maximizing ROI and reducing wasted efforts.

As we conclude this chapter, revenue planning allows CROs and Partner Pros to plan the performance of their partner sales production line. Revenue planning represents the next stage in the evolution of partnership processes and is crucial for addressing the limitations of the traditional program-centric partnering model. Looking ahead, it is anticipated that within the next decade, every CRO and partner leader will be utilizing ChannelOps tools to strategically plan and enhance their ecosystem performance.

Are you revenue planning today? Are you defining metrics and creating revenue plans to guide your PAMs and partners?

MP3-PROCESS
(SALES PRODUCTION LINE)

7

Staying with our production line theme, our MP3 process consists of structured coverage, account mapping, and sales play execution. In the previous phase, the MP3 revenue planning process identified the necessary inputs for our sales acceleration production line, such as active sellers, target accounts, engagement rates, conversion rates, and more. The metrics are used to craft an Execution Plan by Territory and Partner to guarantee the appropriate level of activity needed to achieve the desired revenue goals. Now, it's time to take the ISAM outputs and resource the production line process to generate the desired revenue pipeline output.

In the traditional partnering model, the unit of production is the partner, with all performance metrics measured at the partner level (factory). In the MP3 model, the unit of production shifts to the active seller level (factory floor). This chapter defines the production line process for generating a new pipeline at the seller level, effectively the floor level of the production line.

The MP3 production line is a structured prospecting process that systematically aligns partner sellers with target accounts and resources the prospecting process with sales plays, based on the ISAM outputs, to create our desired outcome new sales pipeline. This comprehensive approach encompasses several key functions, each integral to the partner-led revenue creation process:

- **Strategy Enablement:** Focuses on providing partner sellers with a thorough understanding of the sales strategy tailored to each solution. It centers on training and equipping active sellers with the knowledge and tools to effectively generate demand for your products or services.

- **Account Mapping Process:** This systematic approach identifies and categorizes key target accounts most likely to benefit from the solution. The process goes beyond simply selecting the right accounts; it also involves understanding the specific needs and purchasing behaviors of potential clients within these accounts.

- **Execution Planning:** In this phase, a comprehensive plan is developed detailing how partner sellers will engage with the identified accounts. It includes specifying the sales activities, setting timelines, and outlining the resources required for effective implementation of the solution sales strategy. This plan acts as a roadmap for partner sellers to guide their prospecting efforts.

- **Performance Measurement:** This vital component tracks and analyzes the outcomes of the prospecting activities. It involves measuring key performance indicators such as engagement rates, conversion rates, and overall sales results. Performance measurement is crucial for assessing the effectiveness of the prospecting process and pinpointing areas needing improvement.

Figure 27 outlines our structured target account planning process.

Figure 27.

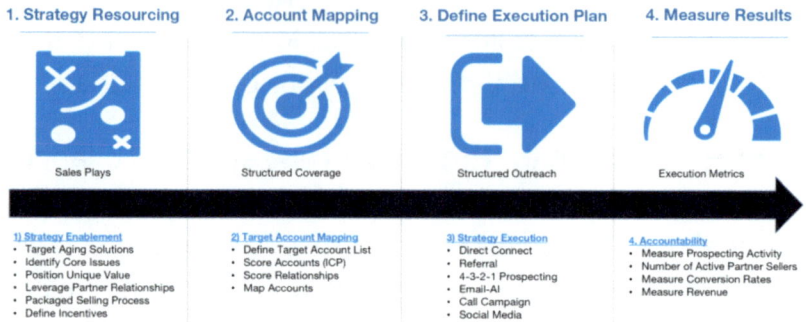

MP3 Target Account Planning Overview

1. Strategy Resourcing	2. Account Mapping	3. Define Execution Plan	4. Measure Results
Sales Plays	Structured Coverage	Structured Outreach	Execution Metrics

1) Strategy Enablement	2) Target Account Mapping	3) Strategy Execution	4. Accountability
• Target Aging Solutions	• Define Target Account List	• Direct Connect	• Measure Prospecting Activity
• Identify Core Issues	• Score Accounts (ICP)	• Referral	• Number of Active Partner Sellers
• Position Unique Value	• Score Relationships	• 4-3-2-1 Prospecting	• Measure Conversion Rates
• Leverage Partner Relationships	• Map Accounts	• Email-AI	• Measure Revenue
• Packaged Selling Process		• Call Campaign	
• Define Incentives		• Social Media	

Transitions Passive Partners To Active Demand Creators

Account mapping complements the MP3 Revenue Planning Process, providing the 'How' to achieve the revenue goals. Moving forward, we will explore each element of our prospecting process, demonstrating how they facilitate the transformation of passive partner sellers into active sellers who are proactively prospecting for your solutions. Throughout this chapter, I will provide a clear understanding of the steps, highlighting how each component contributes to the ultimate goal of sourcing new sales and achieving revenue targets.

One: Strategy Resourcing & Enablement

The first stage of any successful account mapping process is to define what you want sellers to target. We need to identify a pain point and provide a solution to address it. Effective account mapping is not just about aligning common customers between companies; it's about resourcing and executing a sales strategy together.

With resourcing in mind, partners naturally gravitate towards selling solutions that are both easy to sell and profitable. Vendors who streamline the sales process and create impactful incentives effectively cultivate proactive sellers. At the heart of our account mapping process lies solution-based sales plays, which package a comprehensive sales strategy into an easily digestible and executable format.

MP3 sales plays are a recipe for generating sales, providing a clear, step-by-step guide that simplifies selling into manageable actions. These sales plays are designed to align with the solution-specific sales strategy defined in the ISAM process, ensuring that every activity and approach directly contributes to the sales objectives. By breaking down strategies into practical, actionable steps, the process empowers sellers with the tools and clarity they need to navigate account identification, prospecting, customer engagements, sales development, and closing for the win. Structured sales processes ensure consistency and scalability in execution across different partners and market segments delivering increased sales and revenue growth.

In our account mapping process sales plays are aligned to a buyer's journey. This signifies a shift for vendors from relying on generic marketing content and broad product positioning to providing resources tailored to each specific stage of the buyer's evaluation process.

Each sales play within the MP3 framework is constructed like a storyboard, with a clear narrative and objective aimed at resourcing proactive sellers with the tools and strategies needed to progress a buyer through each stage of the sales process. Figure 28 outlines our storyboard process. The content for these plays isn't marketing messaging; it's strategically developed content by roles and responsibilities created to resonate with each persona at every stage of their journey. This methodical approach ensures that the messaging and tactics are tuned to the buyer's needs and mindset at every stage, from awareness and consideration through to decision-making.

The design of MP3 sales plays is underpinned by a deep

understanding of buyer motivations and common objections at each stage of the journey and the specific strategies required to compel the next step in the journey. By focusing on pain points, motivations and outcomes, vendors can equip their partners with powerful content that's not only relevant but highly effective in engaging potential customers. As illustrated the MP3 sales play process provides a clear, structured path for partners to follow, enhancing their ability to generate leads and close sales successfully. This approach ultimately benefits both the vendor and their partners, leading to increased sales and stronger relationships.

Figure 28.

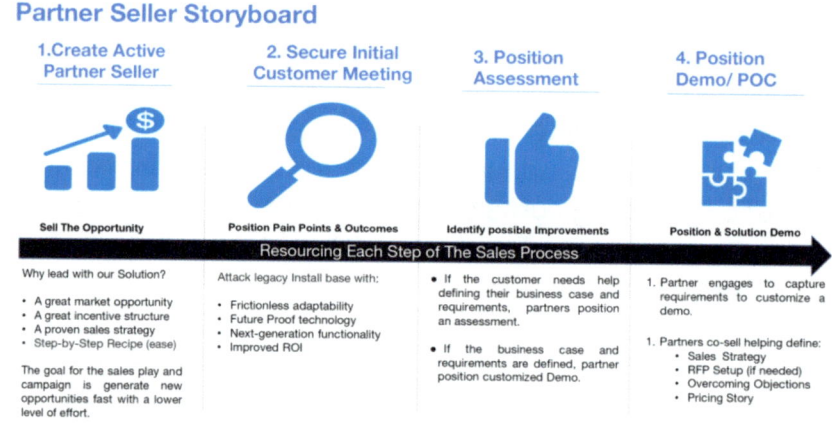

Even though Partner sellers are often seasoned professionals, they benefit from a guide that outlines the strategy and solution-specific steps necessary to generate new sales. Partners tend to gravitate towards vendors that actively contribute to their success. Developing world-class sales playbooks is an excellent way to enhance your relevance and performance with partner sellers. It's important to note that the quality of your sales plays will directly influence the outcomes you achieve. Therefore, invest in crafting strategy-based content and ensure sales plays are enabled with your sellers to maximize their impact. I will cover sales play development and best practices in Chapter 8.

Two: Account Mapping And Territory Planning

Target account mapping is the core of our Sales Production Line Process, serving as the crucial alignment of partners with accounts to optimize market coverage for your solutions. In recent years, various companies have invested heavily in innovating the account mapping process. They have created technology platforms that identify common customers and purchase histories, providing data to pinpoint high-probability accounts at the partnership level for co-selling. These platforms perform well and can be integrated into the MP3 process.

However, MP3 introduces a more comprehensive approach to target account mapping that seamlessly integrates with Revenue Operations (RevOps) planning. Our approach provides more granular targeting, enabling the precise alignment of accounts with the appropriate partners. MP3 account mapping includes several key components:

- **Territory Coverage Planning:** Defines uncovered accounts and assigns a targeted prospecting strategy.

- **Account ICP Scoring:** Identifies high-probability accounts based on solution dynamics to focus efforts where they are most likely to succeed.

- **Relationship Scoring with Economic Buyers:** Maps accounts with the right partners by evaluating the strength of existing relationships.

- **Co-sell Methodology in Account Mapping:** Guides engagements through structured co-sell strategies to enhance collaboration.

- **Account Mapping Policies:** Establishes rules to cycle accounts and minimize channel conflicts, ensuring a smooth operation within the partner ecosystem.

The MP3 process not only provides probability scoring but also layers sales plays to equip partner sellers beyond account identification. In addition, our mapping process can be done manually using a Google database and Data Studio for reports or can be managed through our Salesforce Performance IQ platform, ensuring a structured, data-driven approach to account mapping. Let's delve into the basics of this process.

Territory Planning

Account mapping begins with the broader goal of achieving better account coverage and increased revenue production at a lower cost. This is why companies leverage partnership models. Account mapping should be conducted within a territory coverage strategy that aligns the partner community with a vendor sales manager, aiming to enhance account coverage, boost sales performance, and generate higher commissions.

The initial step in our account mapping process involves defining a target account list by vendor sales territory. This process is designed to aid both the direct sales team and the partner account manager in surpassing their sales targets and fostering co-sell with partner sellers.

Our method includes a straightforward exercise to assess the strength of the relationship between the sellers and the economic buyer within an account. This scoring exercise is done at the named account level for every company. The process starts with a territory list and an assessment is completed that defines:

- **ICP Strength By Solution**- What solutions are a good fit to target for this account? How strong does the account fit our Ideal customer profile?

- **Economic Buyer Identification**- Who is the Economic Buyer for each Solution? Do I know who they are for each account by solution?

- **Relationship Score**- For each targeted account, who has access and what are their relationship scores with targeted economic buyers?

MP3 account mapping is fundamentally a Person-to-Person (P2P) mapping process, not just a Business-to-Business (B2B) approach.

Territory Planning Example

Let's look at a Territory Planning example:

1. **Territory:** 100 Named Accounts

2. **Sales Manager:** 25 Trusted Advisor Relationships Spanning 15 Accounts

3. **Territory Uncovered:** 85 Accounts Uncovered

In our example, the Territory needs effective prospecting coverage for 85 accounts. The Sales Manager has strong coverage for 15 accounts, with trusted advisor or direct relationship scores with 25 economic buyers within these accounts. Typically, the average Sales Manager maintains strategic relationships with fewer than 15 accounts, leaving 85 accounts that require a tailored engagement strategy.

To address these gaps, our methodology leverages partners and their networks to gain access. Partner Managers align the 85 open accounts with the partner community through a formal target account mapping process and replicate the relationship scoring exercise. This collaborative effort systematically reduces the number of open accounts as we progress through the mapping process. In addition, Partners are asked to add to the list based on their accounts and trusted advisor relationships.

For accounts in white space—areas where we lack partner coverage—we proactively recruit new partners with access to the economic buyer in these unpenetrated accounts.

Note: I use PartnerOptimizer (www.partneroptimizer.com) to identify potential partners for recruitment. Additionally, we initiate account-based marketing campaigns to raise awareness and generate interest, ensuring comprehensive coverage and engagement across all potential accounts in the territory. Figure 29 provides a sample account list from Salesforce.

Figure 29.

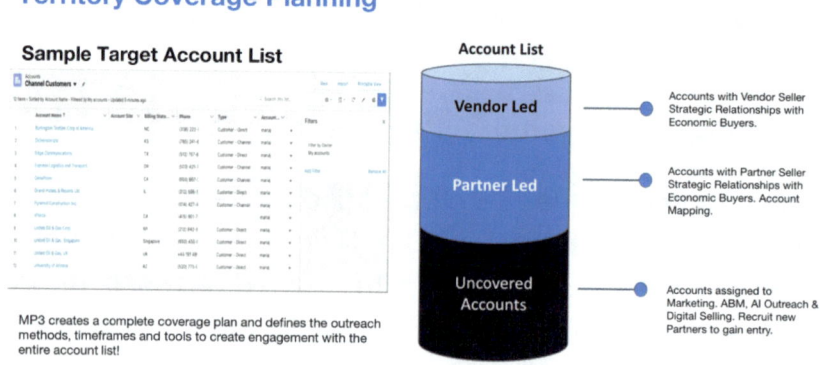

107

Territory planning and partner account mapping based on relationship scores provide several key benefits that enhance the effectiveness and efficiency of sales strategies:

- **Better Alignment:** Ensures a seamless integration between the partner community and direct sales teams, fostering cooperation and synchronized efforts.

- **Enhanced Account Coverage:** Strategic positioning of sales resources leads to more comprehensive coverage of accounts.

- **Deeper Account Penetration:** Focuses efforts on high-potential accounts, maximizing the impact and reach within these key areas.

- **Improved Opportunity Pipeline:** Targeted account mapping results in a more robust pipeline of sales opportunities.

- **Greater Commissions:** Increased sales efficiency and success in targeted areas lead to higher commissions for sales teams.

- **Enhanced Measurement and Accountability:** Provides a clear framework for tracking the execution of channel strategies, improving accountability across teams.

- **Optimized Resource Utilization:** Ensures that sales and partner resources are deployed strategically to maximize effectiveness and outcomes.

More importantly, Territory Planning and Account Mapping bring direct sellers, partners, and partnering organizations together under a unified co-sell framework. This ensures comprehensive Territory Plans that include clear measurement and accountability. Additionally, this approach establishes a cohesive team with well-defined roles and responsibilities.

Note: Territory Account Planning introduces the broader discussion of direct sales, channel sales, or hybrid models. Additionally, there's often a reluctance to address compensation issues, such as whether to use double or single compensation schemes. While these are valid concerns, it's important to recognize that the benefits derived from territory planning and partner-sourced revenue generally surpass those of a direct-only sales model. Partners often own strategic relationships and have influence in longstanding accounts. The acceleration to market and revenue gains achieved when partners are prospecting on your behalf typically far exceed the time-to-value and costs associated with partner sales.

Account Mapping Scoring Process

Account Mapping, the third phase in our prospecting process, plays a critical role in establishing a successful sales strategy. When executed effectively, account mapping offers a structured coverage model that guarantees comprehensive market reach, focusing on high-probability accounts. This phase is instrumental in ensuring that the targeted accounts are appropriately aligned with the most suitable partners, enhancing the overall effectiveness of the sales efforts.

The following is the method I teach for pinpointing the highest probability accounts and correctly assigning those accounts to the right partners. While there are several excellent mapping tools available from companies like Crossbeam, Reveal, and PartnerTap, our approach offers a methodology for scoring accounts and relationships, incorporating a probability dimension into the account mapping process. This additional layer enhances the precision and effectiveness of the mapping process.

Scoring Accounts

The adoption of a data-driven account identification and assignment process is key to this phase. It not only improves engagement rates by ensuring that partners are focusing on the right accounts but also significantly increases the likelihood of progressing these engagements into tangible opportunities. This strategic alignment between accounts and partners leads to a more efficient and productive sales process, where efforts are concentrated on the most promising prospects, thereby maximizing the potential for successful outcomes. The initial and perhaps most crucial step in the target account planning process is the accurate identification of high-probability accounts that stand to gain significantly from implementing your solution. Achieving sales efficiency hinges on targeting the right accounts that align with your solution's strengths and potential benefits. A common pitfall in many target account mapping processes is the misalignment of accounts with the solutions offered, leading to inefficient and unproductive sales efforts.

Consider a straightforward, if somewhat exaggerated, example: marketing the best snowmobile in the industry to accounts in Florida is an exercise in futility. This example, while hyperbolic, drives home an important point. It's essential to avoid directing partner sellers' efforts towards pursuing accounts that have little chance of success due to a fundamental mismatch between the product and the target market.

To circumvent this issue, the account mapping process should begin with a clear definition of an Ideal Customer Profile (ICP) for your solutions. This profile should encompass a range of attributes and characteristics that define the most suitable and potentially profitable customers for what you are offering. By establishing this profile, you can ensure that your partner sellers are focused on pursuing accounts that are not only likely to be interested in your solutions but also have a higher probability of converting into successful sales. This targeted approach is key to maximizing the efficiency and effectiveness of your sales efforts.

The MP3 targeting process utilizes a strategic approach known as the "Five I's" to develop a comprehensive Ideal Customer Profile (ICP). This method ensures that the focus is on accounts with the highest probability of successful engagement and conversion. Here's a breakdown of the five I's:

- **Identify the Issues (Score 20):** Determine the specific problems or challenges that your solution is designed to address. This can also be a defined market opportunity. Understanding these issues is crucial to align your offering with the needs of potential customers.

- **Identify the Initiative (Score 20):** Pinpoint the initiatives or goals that your solution supports. This involves recognizing broader organizational objectives or projects that your solution can contribute to or enhance.

- **Identify the Industries (Score 20):** Target industries that are most relevant to the issues your solution addresses and the initiatives it supports. This step is about aligning your solution with sectors that are most likely to benefit from what you offer.

- **Identify Targeted Individuals (Score 20):** Determine who the decision-makers or key influencers are within these industries. These are the individuals who have the authority or influence to decide on or advocate for your solution.

- **Define the Install-Base Legacy Solutions (Score 20):** Identify the existing or legacy solutions that your product is positioned to replace. Understanding what you are up against or what you are offering as an alternative can help refine your targeting strategy.

As you build your ICP and scoring process you can weight elements that are the highest priority or use a straight average approach. Once you have developed your ICP scoring model, each account should be scored against the ICP criteria for a solution, providing a quantifiable method to identify high-probability accounts. This scoring system offers a clear reference point, enabling the efficient and effective prioritization of accounts most likely to yield successful engagements and sales conversions. This methodical approach ensures that prospecting efforts are targeted to the most promising opportunities.

Note: The Five I's provide a straightforward process for developing an Ideal Customer Profile (ICP), offering criteria for scoring accounts to pinpoint the most promising targets for engagement. This method focuses on identifying accounts with a high likelihood of success, aiming to enhance sales efficiency. However, it's important to remember that you're not limited to using the Five I's as your scoring criteria. You can incorporate your own ICP elements, such as company size, financial capacity, solution upgrade opportunities and other relevant factors. The crucial aspect of our scoring process is the total ICP score must sum up to 100 for plotting purposes. See Figure 30.

Scoring Partner Relationships

Scoring relationships is a pivotal component for an efficient target account planning process, helping to elevate engagement rates. Our process uses relationship scores to map accounts and establish a clear understanding of the partner sellers' ability to generate an initial meeting with a targeted economic buyer. We employ a comprehensive scoring key with the following Relationship Scoring Definitions:

■ **Trusted Advisor (Score 100):** This designation signifies a relationship of utmost importance, where you hold the role of a trusted advisor, wielding substantial influence within the account.

■ **Direct Access (Score 80):** An association characterized by direct engagement and situational influence, often specific to a particular function and typically reactive in nature.

■ **Referral Access (Score 60):** You possess a relationship with an influencer within the account who holds the capacity to refer you to the Economic Buyer, adding a significant layer of access and influence.

■ **Email Access (Score 40):** This level entails modest access, primarily through email or social media channels, with stakeholders, albeit lacking substantial influence.

■ **No Access (Score 20):** The lowest rating, indicative of undefined access and a lack of any discernible relationship or pertinent information to identify the Economic buyer or Decision Maker(s).

These well-defined relationship scoring definitions serve as the compass guiding account assignments. The combination of ICP score and Relationship Score helps you plot accounts and prioritize engagement. Plotting helps you define the probability of generating an initial meeting. See Figure 30.

Figure 30.

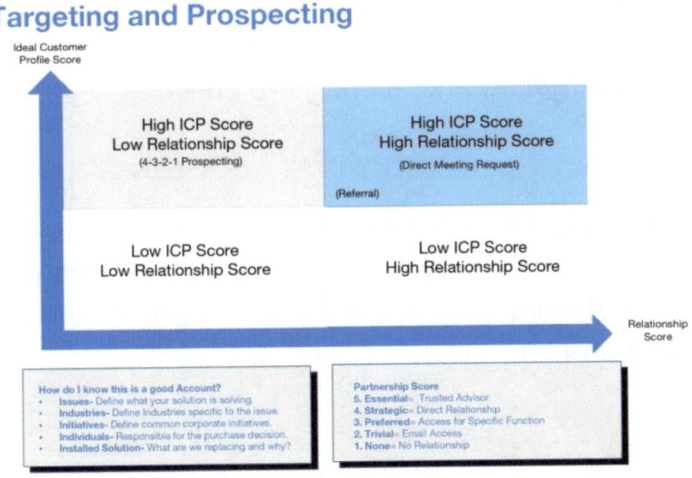

Targeting and Prospecting

Ideal Customer Profile Score

High ICP Score Low Relationship Score (4-3-2-1 Prospecting)	High ICP Score High Relationship Score (Direct Meeting Request) (Referral)
Low ICP Score Low Relationship Score	Low ICP Score High Relationship Score

Relationship Score

How do I know this is a good Account?
- **Issues-** Define what your solution is solving.
- **Industries-** Define industries specific to the issue.
- **Initiatives-** Define common corporate initiatives.
- **Individuals-** Responsible for the purchase decision.
- **Installed Solution-** What are we replacing and why?

Partnership Score
5. **Essential-** Trusted Advisor
4. **Strategic-** Direct Relationship
3. **Preferred-** Access for Specific Function
2. **Trivial-** Email Access
1. **None-** No Relationship

The success of your target account mapping process is heavily reliant on the accurate identification and alignment of both accounts and partner sellers. Identifying the right accounts and effectively mapping them, coupled with the enablement of a well-crafted sales play, lays a solid foundation for effective prospecting and client engagement. The importance of diligently scoring and prioritizing accounts and sellers is fundamental to this process. This careful evaluation ensures that efforts are strategically focused on the most promising prospects and that partner sellers are well-equipped to engage these targets effectively. A comprehensive approach is essential for a successful and productive sales endeavor, maximizing the potential for positive outcomes and efficient use of resources.

Note: Identifying and scoring accounts is the "call to action" for every enablement session. Partner managers work with partner sellers to score and plot accounts, picking the best four accounts from each seller to target together for the quarter. The goal is to create engagements fast. If your targeting process and sales plays produce meetings that transition to sales, partner sellers will run your sales play over and over. Conversely, if you fail to produce in the first account mapping session, sellers will revert to opportunistic behaviors. This is why proper targeting and scoring are critical.

Three: Execution Planning (Account Mapping)

Now that you have defined and resourced the sales play you want to run and completed your territory coverage plan by mapping and identifying accounts to assign, it's time to define the execution plan. What actions do I want partner sellers to take?

The MP3 Target Account Planning is a strategic approach to sales coverage that harnesses the strength of our partner community to reach our intended target market. Target account planning is a comprehensive execution strategy that connects the value of our solutions with the needs of the market. When executed effectively, Target account planning transforms our sales, channel sales, and partner network into a demand-generation engine, creating consistent brand awareness and accelerating sales. Implementing a structured target account planning process offers numerous benefits to both our internal sales teams and partners.

- Partners benefit from a step-by-step sales creation process that maps the value of our solutions to market needs. They are rewarded for sales development efforts and can access higher-level incentives.

- Vendor sales teams benefit as partners transition from mere fulfillment to active demand creation. This transition enhances our coverage of target accounts and drives increased sales.

- Channel sales benefit from strategic alignment and increased relevance within the partner community.

Additionally, they gain visibility into ecosystem strategy execution performance.

To achieve these benefits you will need to plan your target account mapping workflow. Figure 31 defines our enablement workflow.

Figure 31.

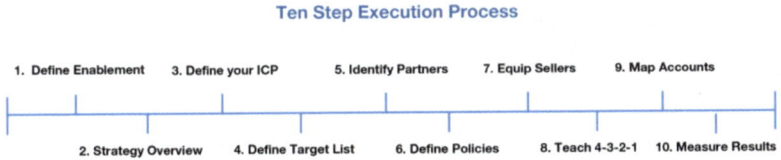

Account Mapping Execution Planning (Workflow)

Ten Step Execution Process

1. Define Enablement   3. Define your ICP   5. Identify Partners   7. Equip Sellers   9. Map Accounts

2. Strategy Overview   4. Define Target List   6. Define Policies   8. Teach 4-3-2-1   10. Measure Results

Repeat This Process With Each Impact Partner Quarterly!

Step 1. Plan Your Strategy Enablement

Planning starts with a sales enablement session. This session is designed to equip partners with the knowledge and tools they need to generate new solution leads rapidly.

Best Practice: Before hosting a partner enablement session, be sure to do your homework and come ready to provide a sales play overview, teach the target account mapping process, and work with your partners on defining and mapping high probability accounts with your sales teams.

Step 2. Solution & Sales Play Overview

Plan a concise 10-minute overview of your solution, focusing on identifying the market need and the sales opportunities it addresses. This understanding helps sellers align the solution

116

with current market priorities and demonstrates its relevance to potential customers. The objective of the sales play overview is to highlight the importance of your solution, motivating sellers to become active advocates who confidently present your offering to their clients. Additionally, this review will familiarize participants with the strategic approach to selling the product, guiding them through each stage of the sales process. This not only boosts their confidence in the solution but also enhances their capability to effectively position and sell it.

Best Practice: I recommend that CAMs offer two formats for sales play enablement to accommodate different learning preferences and schedules:

■ Deliver live training for both sales teams and partner presales engineers. This method facilitates real-time interaction and immediate feedback, enhancing the learning experience.

■ Provide a recorded online version of the sales play training, accessible through your partner portal or website. This option allows for flexibility, giving participants the ability to learn at their own pace and revisit the material as needed.

These dual options ensure that training is both flexible and accessible, catering to those who prefer self-directed learning as well as those who benefit from more interactive, personal training sessions.

Step 3. Create An Ideal Customer Profile (ICP)

Account mapping is a standard practice for aligning accounts with partners when introducing new vendor solutions. However, many account mapping processes do not include a specific target profile for partners, which is crucial for effective opportunity qualification. Creating a target profile is vital as it helps define and qualify your target market, allowing partner sales teams to quickly and efficiently identify accounts that are a good fit. This targeted profiling enables partners to rapidly pinpoint opportunities that align well with our solution sales play, streamlining the process of matching solutions to potential clients. Use the ICP development and scoring process outlined earlier to target accounts.

Best Practice: The ICP serves as a guideline rather than a strict rule. Its primary purpose is to identify accounts with a high probability of success. Feel free to adjust the ICP to better match the customer base of each partner, ensuring it remains relevant and effective for different contexts.

Step 4. Create A Territory Target Account List

Before assigning accounts to partners, each vendor sales team collaborates with channel sales to create a target account list based on the target profile and available accounts that the vendor territory manager is looking to access. Developing this list by territory and prioritizing it forms the master list, which we can use to assign partners to accounts. In addition, partners will bring accounts to be added to the list. Developing a master target account list is a collaborative process. Each territory sales team keeps track of its master list to manage assignments and identify coverage gaps. In many cases, a company CRM acts as the repository for the target account lists and assignments.

Best Practice: Partners often have a broader reach into accounts over vendors, primarily because their solutions are more diverse and impact a wider range of individuals and organizations within a client's company. Utilizing the target account planning process allows you to leverage extensive partner knowledge to gain insights about accounts, economic buyers, and ongoing initiatives. This significantly enhances both the quality and depth of your target account information.

Partners are invaluable resources for enriching your target account list and deepening your understanding of each account's specific needs and opportunities.

Step 5. Identify Partner Coverage

To determine which partners are most likely to succeed with our target account planning process, channel sales must assess partnerships based on their ability to access the intended target market and execute our sales strategy effectively. This assessment helps to evaluate a partner's potential to positively impact sales.

In our model, partners are valued for their ability to reach target customers, their commitment to selling the solution, their combined sales and technical expertise in relation to the solution, and their performance in generating demand with minimal support. The strength of a partner should be reflected in these key areas:

- **Solution Competency**: Their ability to independently generate and close sales of the solution.

- **Target Market Reach**: Their effectiveness in connecting our solution with the target market.

- **Program Level**: Their commitment to and performance in our partner program, which may include price advantages.

- **Sales Priority**: The priority given to our solutions relative to other products the partner sells.

Stack ranking partners based on demand creation criteria provides a fresh perspective on the strength of your partners and the overall health of your channel. Here's a straightforward formula to evaluate the strength of your partners to generate demand.

Score each of our impact elements using the following scale (High=10, Medium=5, Low=0).

1. **Competency** of your partners.
2. **Target Market Reach** for your solution.
3. **Program Level Attainment.**
4. **Sales Priority** to sell your solution.

Total and divide by 4 and use the following scale:

- **High Impact**: 35-40.

- **Favorable**: 30.

- **Low**: Less than 30.

Partner Impact scores are aligned with the revenue planning process highlighted in Chapter 6. As our Planning IQ software produces the metrics required to achieve the revenue target, one of these metrics defines the number of partners needed to achieve the goal. Partner Impact scores are used to identify the top partners to implement your target account planning process.

Best Practice: Partner Impact Scoring is also a useful method for evaluating individual partner sellers. Begin by creating a list of known sellers and assess them based on three key criteria: their ability to reach your target market, the priority they assign to executing your sales play, and their competency in selling your solution. I recommend organizing this into a three-tiered list, identifying the top 40 sellers as your primary focus, followed by the next 20 sellers whom you aim to develop into champions, and then anybody else. This structured list should guide where you allocate your engagement and resources, allowing you to prioritize your efforts effectively to create active sellers.

Note: Tools from companies like Crossbeam, Reveal, and PartnerTap can effectively replace this part of the process. They excel at identifying and leveraging existing relationships for mutual engagement.

Step 6. Define Process, Policies & Incentives

Define your Target Account Mapping policies and incentives before approaching partners with the structured coverage model. Some considerations include the length of time to assign an account, deal registration policies, channel conflict policies, etc.

Best Practices: Here are some best practices for effective policy management:

- **Assign Accounts Temporarily:** Allocate accounts to partners for a 90-day prospecting period. If the partner demonstrates progress, consider extending their assignment for an additional 90 days.

- **Protect Partner Efforts:** Implement deal registration to safeguard the prospecting efforts of partners. If a partner is assigned an account for a specific solution sales play, ensure that any deal registrations for that solution are credited to them during their assignment period. This protection is crucial as it motivates partners to engage in prospecting activities.

- **Rotate Accounts Strategically:** If a partner shows no progress with an account, consider rotating it to another partner. However, it is important to clearly outline your account rotation policies during enablement sessions to maintain transparency and manage expectations.

- **Incentivize Key Activities:** Develop incentives for partners who achieve specific milestones, such as generating meetings. These incentives encourage active engagement and are instrumental in driving sales outcomes.

Documenting and educating partners on your policies is essential to build a healthy and productive partner ecosystem. Proper policy alignment reduces channel conflict!

Step 7. Equip Sellers (Enablement)

In many account mapping exercises, partners may not be adequately trained or equipped to execute a structured sales play. Equipping Sellers with the necessary tools, resources, and processes is essential for generating new opportunities. This empowers partners to navigate target customers through the sales development process.

Best Practice: Thoroughly train partner sellers on the entire sales play, including specific messaging, emails, call scripts, qualification questions, pitch deck, deal registration process, demo procedures, sales development support, handling common objections, incentives, and potential expansion opportunities. Partner sellers who are well-trained and equipped consistently outperform those who are not, achieving better results 100% of the time. This strategic enablement training not only shows your commitment to their success but also establishes immediate credibility by demonstrating that every aspect of the sales process has been carefully planned and defined.

Step 8. Define Sales Actions (4-3-2-1)

Collaborate with each seller to pinpoint four accounts that have the highest probability of success, based on your ICP and their relationship scores with economic buyers. Have partner sellers reach out to arrange meetings. Apply the 4-3-2-1 prospecting methodology, detailed in Chapter 4 page 38, which focuses on leveraging direct relationships or referral relationships to create engagement. This targeted approach enhances the effectiveness of your engagement strategies.

Best Practice: Prospecting is often the least favorite activity among sales teams. Many companies now delegate cold outreach tasks to Sales Development Representatives (SDRs), commonly known as inside sales teams, to generate sales-qualified leads for Account Managers. However, leveraging existing relationships remains the fastest and most efficient method to build a sales pipeline. The 4-3-2-1 Prospecting Process is designed to maximize efficiency in every step. This method emphasizes the high rewards of following a straightforward process that requires no more than 10 minutes per day to implement. By selling the favorable reward-to-effort ratio of the 4-3-2-1 Prospecting Process, sales teams can see significant returns with minimal daily investment.

Step 9. Map & Align Co-Sell Engagement

Score accounts and pinpoint those with high potential for each partner seller. Verify these accounts against your master list to ensure they are not already assigned to another partner. Facilitate an introductory email or arrange a call to align the direct account owner with the partner seller. This coordination helps to secure an agreement, exchange account details, and establish a clear prospecting plan.

Best Practice: Invite your direct sellers to your account mapping calls to align account assignments in a single meeting. The account alignment and information exchange phase of account mapping is crucial. I teach a three-step process with sign-off to ensure co-sell activities are fully coordinated:

- **Vendor Account Owner** - Partner Seller Introduction.

- **Information Exchange:** Use a simple checklist to guide these conversations. Both vendor and partner should answer these questions to foster collaboration:

  1. What's the state of the account?
  2. Who do you know?
  3. What are the relevant company or organizational initiatives?
  4. What is the Engagement Plan?
  5. Timeframes? Targeted Contacts?
  6. What can I do to support you with your strategic goals?
  7. What else do I need to know?

- **Communication Cadence:** Decide when and how often to connect. Follow up with an email to document the agreement.

Step 10. Implement Performance Analytics

Performance analytics must be incorporated into the Target Account Planning process to measure progress and facilitate course corrections in our Execution Plan. Measurement and accountability are vital components. It's crucial to define the evolution of channel metrics, data capture, and real-time channel metrics for accurate tracking and reporting Chapter 10 is dedicated to Territory Management of the MP3 Target Account Mapping process.

Best Practice: Conduct this process quarterly with your high-impact partners and sellers. Partners appreciate knowing that you are dedicated to the established processes. By regularly engaging in this way, you will expand your pool of active sellers as they experience successful outcomes from executing the sales play. Conversely, if we fail to help our partners succeed with our strategy, they may seek opportunities elsewhere. Regular engagement and support are crucial for maintaining strong partner relationships and mutual success.

Four: Measure Mapping Results

The final phase of our target account mapping process is to measure results. I cover how to measure the results of the MP3 target account planning process in detail in both Chapter 9, "MP3 Performance Management," and Chapter 10, "Territory Management."

Conclusion

The core of MP3 production line is a structured prospecting process that systematically aligns partner sellers with target accounts and resources the prospecting process with sales plays, based on the ISAM outputs, to create our desired outcome: new sales pipeline. This comprehensive approach encompasses several key functions, each integral to the partner-led revenue creation process, including:

- Strategy Enablement

- Account Mapping

- Execution Planning

- Performance Measurement

By systematically equipping partner sellers with the necessary tools and clear processes, the you can ensure that each element of your sales strategy is effectively executed. This structured yet flexible framework empowers partners to maximize their sales potential, resulting in increased revenue and stronger market presence.

Finally, adopting our ten-step process provides a straightforward workflow to streamline your target account planning process. Developing a consistent approach and establishing clear policies for target account mapping enables you to expand your account coverage and quickly increase the number of active sellers. Ensuring alignment is crucial to minimizing conflicts and enhancing efficiency to produce results.

Chapter Application

One of the key elements to revenue growth is providing partner sellers with a clear and actionable execution plan. A good target account mapping process, defined by methodology, creates a compelling opportunity to structure the sellers' go-to-market activities and establish the right level of coverage and controls to deliver revenue growth. Here are some actionable things for CROs and Partner Pros to consider:

One: Align Your Target Account Planning Process: Incorporate this as part of a territory coverage plan for each vendor seller. Define all the accounts in a territory that meet your ICP and score relationships to identify the route to the economic buyer. Assign accounts based on relationships.

Two: Create a Storyboard: Define the workflow for creating new sales. The storyboard will outline each step of your sales process, the pain points, buying motivations, and common objections at each stage. Determine what's needed to progress the buyer to the next stage and build your enablement and sales plays to accommodate the process.

Three: Plan Your Target Account Planning Process: Ensure you walk through each stage and have your policies, processes, and training ready so partner sellers can hit the ground running.

Four: **Measure Strategy Execution Performance**: Evaluate performance at both the account and seller levels to ensure your strategies are effective.

Adopting and resourcing a formal account mapping process is essential to effectively leverage partner relationships and speed time-to-value. Equipping partner sellers with sales plays will dramatically improve their sales efficiency and win rates. Chapter 8 explores what's needed to build effective sales plays that your partner sellers will actually use!

MP3 SALES PLAY DEVELOPMENT

8

The effectiveness of your sales acceleration production line hinges on the quality of inputs (partner sellers) and the robustness of your pipeline production process (prospecting). The MP3 process is designed to bridge the selling skills gap of partner sellers while enhancing the outcomes produced by your sales strategy and partner execution. To facilitate proper execution, MP3 employs sales plays that provide a simple, step-by-step guide for partner sellers to follow. Much like any endeavor in life, the caliber of your sales play and the thoroughness of your enablement efforts will directly influence the performance of the seller. In this chapter, we will discuss best practices for developing high-performance sales plays that transform passive sellers into active, results-driven sellers.

This chapter outlines the fundamental techniques used by Channel Force Inc. to craft advanced sales plays that generate active sellers and inspire economic buyers to action. Sales plays are essential for guiding the target account mapping and prospecting activities that are part of the MP3-Process phase of the model. However, the depth and breadth of the production line element of our model is too extensive to be covered in a single chapter. So I have broken the MP3-Process into two chapters. Since we have covered account mapping, let's focus on how to develop winning sales plays to complement the prospecting and sales development process.

Sales Play Considerations

Before diving into best practices, let's first outline what constitutes an effective sales play. Sales plays should be crafted based on the complexity of your solution's sales process and the specific outcomes you aim to achieve. A robust sales play considers the buyer's needs, their purchase decision journey, the vendor's sales process, and the goals and solutions of the partners. The sales play serves as a centralized strategy to standardize the selling process for a solution, creating a repeatable and scalable method that can be effectively implemented across the entire partner ecosystem.

Although numerous companies employ sales plays, there's a significant distinction between a high-performance sales play, which offers a data-driven, step-by-step guide for executing sales prospecting and opportunity development strategies that generate new sales, and marketing plays. The effectiveness of your sellers' prospecting efforts hinges on the quality of your solution sales play. The MP3 sales play development process is an extensive methodology that integrates insights from sales, customers, marketing, and industry data to craft a thoroughly packaged selling process that anticipates the buyers' motivations and objections leading to a highly tuned recipe for success.

MP3 Sales Play Benefits

An MP3 Sales Play offers several advantages over a standard marketing document, particularly in terms of strategic execution and practical application. Here are four key benefits:

- **Data-Driven Strategy**: The MP3 Sales Play is grounded in data, incorporating insights from various sources such as sales performance, customer feedback, marketing analytics, and industry trends. This approach ensures that strategies are not only theoretically sound but also tested and refined based on real-world data, leading to more predictable and successful outcomes.

- **Step-by-Step Execution Guide**: Unlike a marketing document, which often provides general guidance and promotional content, an MP3 Sales Play includes a detailed, step-by-step action plan. This makes it easier for sales teams to understand and follow through with specific actions needed to drive sales, reducing ambiguity and enhancing the efficiency of sales initiatives.

- **Integrated Insights:** By utilizing insights from multiple facets of the business—including sales, customer behavior, marketing, and industry-specific data—the MP3 Sales Play offers a holistic view of the sales landscape. This integration helps in creating a more cohesive and comprehensive sales strategy that aligns with broader business objectives and market demands.

- **Customized Selling Processes:** The MP3 Sales Play is tailored to meet the specific needs of the organization and its target customer base, which differs significantly from generic marketing materials. This customization ensures that the sales strategies are relevant and effectively address the unique challenges and opportunities within the targeted market segments.

These benefits make the MP3 Sales Play a more effective tool for driving sales and improving the overall performance of sales teams compared to traditional marketing documents.

Sales Play Best Practices

Here is the methodology I use to develop Sales Plays for my clients. This section outlines the process and best practices necessary for creating effective sales plays that partner sellers will actively use. Remember, sales plays serve two primary functions:

1. Transforming passive sellers into active prospectors.

2. Resourcing the typical buyer's journey for a solution, thereby constructing a process that educates, convinces, and compels economic buyers to engage.

Sales plays are essentially the recipes that catalyze action for both sellers and buyers! As you look to build Sales Plays, let's walk through eight best practices I use to build high-performance sales plays.

One: Take Inventory Of Your Process

The development of a Sales Play begins with creating a blueprint. A robust sales play identifies a market opportunity and outlines a tested sales process to seize that opportunity effectively. In the MP3 approach, we craft our sales plays like a recipe, providing clear, step-by-step instructions and guidelines. Figure 32 outlines the process starting with an inventory check of the necessary components. Here are the key elements of our sales play:

- **A Clearly Identified Market Need:** This refers to a specific, recognized demand or problem in the market that the sales play intends to address. Identifying a market need involves understanding what gaps exist in the current market offerings and how potential customers will benefit from a new or improved product or service.

- **Ideal Customer Profiles by Persona:** These profiles are detailed descriptions of the economic buyers for your solution. Each persona is based on market research and real data about customer demographics, behavior patterns, buying motivations, and goals. Creating these profiles helps in tailoring sales and marketing strategies to meet the specific needs of different customer segments.

- **Value Propositions Tailored for Each Persona:** A value proposition is a clear statement that explains how a product or service solves customers' priority problems or improves their situation (i.e., delivers specific benefits). Tailoring these value propositions for each persona ensures that the messaging resonates more deeply with varied customer needs and expectations, emphasizing how the offering is relevant to each specific group.

- **Solution Outcomes that the Sales Play Aims to Achieve:** These are the expected results or benefits that the product or service aims to deliver through the sales play. Solution outcomes are typically framed in terms of how they help the customer overcome challenges or achieve goals, and they are crucial for demonstrating the effectiveness of the product or service.

- **Buyer's Journey Mapped Out by Stage:** The buyer's journey is the process buyers go through to become aware of, consider and evaluate, and decide to purchase a new product or service. Mapping this out by stage (awareness, consideration, decision) helps sales and marketing teams develop targeted strategies that align with where the customer is in their purchasing process.

- **Detailed Sales Strategy and Actions for Each Stage:** This component involves outlining specific strategies and actions that sales teams should take at each stage of the buyer's journey to effectively guide potential customers toward making a purchase. This could include tactics for initial contact, follow-up, demonstration of products, negotiation, and closing.

- **Necessary Activities to be Completed Throughout the Process:** These are the tasks and steps that must be carried out to implement the sales strategy effectively. This can include activities like lead generation, engagement initiatives, follow-up meetings, and administrative tasks like data entry and reporting.

- **Benefits for Both the Seller and the Customer:** This refers to the advantages each party gains from the transaction. For the customer, benefits might include solving a problem, enhancing productivity, or improving quality of life. For the seller, benefits typically include financial gain, increased market share, and enhanced customer relationships.

Gathering and organizing these elements are crucial for planning the sales play and defining its structure. This structured approach ensures that every step of the sales process is aligned with both the market demands and the strategic goals of the organization.

Figure 32.

MP3 Sales Play Development Considerations & Checklist

Two: Build To The Buyer's Journey

A well-crafted sales play acts as a recipe that guides sellers on how to generate new leads effectively. A structured performance sales play provides a step-by-step guide, equipping any seller with the necessary resources, skills, and processes to generate new demand and nurture leads from the initial meeting through to closing the sale and beyond.

One best practice involves aligning the buyer's journey with your sales process to clearly define the steps a customer will progress through. By understanding and anticipating your buyer's discovery, decision-making processes, and the steps needed to validate and close the deal, you can create tailored messaging and resources to address potential challenges and accelerate the sales cycle. Figure 33 represents a simple sales process workflow for a SaaS Company.

Figure 33.

Consider each step of your sales process and what is expected of the customer. Think about the typical questions you ask or receive, the common objections you need to address, the features or use cases that consistently lead to sales, why they are effective, and what should be avoided when selling the solution. The answers to these questions for each stage of the process aid in developing a consistent selling motion, which is crucial for transferring knowledge to partner sellers.

Three: Creating Compelling Messaging

A good sales play provides sellers with the tools they need for effective outreach. Earlier, we introduced the 4-3-2-1 Prospecting Process, which is designed to create six touchpoints and nurture the prospect over a three-week period to foster engagement. The 4-3-2-1 process comprises four key elements:

- **Equipping Sellers with an Elevator Pitch:** Prepare sellers with a concise, persuasive pitch that clearly articulates the value proposition of your product or service in a way that resonates quickly with potential clients.

- **Providing Sellers with Compelling Sequenced Messaging:** Supply sellers with well-crafted Messaging templates that capture attention, convey key messages effectively, and encourage responses or further conversation. (Email, Linkedin, Social Media, etc.)

- **Developing Compelling Call Scripts**: Create detailed call scripts that guide sellers through phone interactions, ensuring they convey the necessary points, handle objections skillfully, and keep the conversation moving toward a positive outcome.

- **Leveraging Referrals:** Encourage sellers to use referrals effectively, as they can significantly enhance credibility and open doors that might otherwise remain closed.

- **Use Automation and Digital Selling Technology:** When possible leverage technologies like digital selling and automated outreach technologies to complement your outreach approach.

As you develop your sales plays, it's crucial to address each of these elements thoroughly. Let's explore some best practices for each area to ensure your sales team is well-prepared and effective in their prospecting efforts.

Develop a Compelling Value Proposition

Craft a value proposition that quickly identifies a common pain point and offers a clear, tangible solution. For example, many IT organizations are struggling to manage a high volume of trouble tickets while controlling IT budget expenses. A good pitch might be:

"Many IT departments are facing challenges in managing their trouble tickets and keeping costs under control. Could we schedule a 30-minute meeting if I could demonstrate how our cost-effective network automation tool is helping our customers reduce their network trouble tickets by 95% and cut their support costs by an average of 40%?"

This approach directly addresses a significant issue and presents a clear, quantifiable benefit, making it a compelling reason for a meeting. There was no mention of a product, just a problem statement, an outcome that can be created, and an offer to learn more. Effective value propositions should be simple and to the point!

Develop a Compelling Outreach Sequence

Our approach involves crafting a series of outreaches that effectively engage the prospect throughout the buying process. This sequence includes an introduction, an objection-handling message, and an offer. Below are examples of each type of outreach in our sequence:

- **Introduction Outreach:** This initial outreach aims to define a problem and the core benefits of your solution. The focus is on capturing interest and establishing relevance. For example:

"[Name], 90% of IT organizations are challenged with [common problems]. If I could show you how to produce [outcome/benefit/result], would you give me 30 minutes of your time? [partner name] and I have successfully helped [their title] achieve [specific outcome] with companies like [company]." Let me know your thoughts.

- **Objection-Handling Outreach:** This email anticipates and addresses common objections that prospects might have. It should provide additional information to reassure the prospect and solidify the value of your solution. For example:

"[Name], I know how busy you are, but if you could spare 30 minutes, I would love to show you a solution for [problem] that *is producing [statistics/benefit/result]. I promise I won't waste* your time."

- **Offer Outreach:** The final email in the sequence makes a compelling offer or calls to action that encourages the prospect to make a decision. For example:

"[Name], social proof is what everyone is looking for, but I will *do one better. I'd like to offer you [free trial/ebook/training] so* you can see firsthand the impact [solution] will have on solving [problem]. [company] deployed our solution and achieved [outcome] result. If you are not the right person, is there someone else I should speak with?"

Each email is designed to build on the previous one, effectively guiding the prospect through the decision-making process toward making a commitment. While today's AI technologies can assist in generating high-quality emails, it's crucial to keep them concise, focused, and customer-centric. The sequence I advocate involves messaging around the problem, the desired outcome, the solution, and the path forward—a logical progression that naturally leads to a discussion.

Additionally, it's important to allow space in your email sequence for partners to communicate their own value and personalize the branding of the email. This helps in aligning the content with their unique voice and enhances the partnership feel of the communication. Lastly, crafting compelling email subject lines is an art form that can significantly boost open rates. I utilize online tools like SendCheckIt to score subject lines. There are numerous free tools available online that you can use to evaluate and improve your subject lines, which you can find by searching for "subject line scores" on search engines. This step is key in ensuring your emails stand out and get noticed in crowded inboxes.

Leverage Referrals

Encouraging sellers to use referrals is a crucial step in connecting with economic buyers, who are key decision-makers in most B2B sales processes. Since buying decisions often involve multiple stakeholders, getting a referral to one economic buyer is just the beginning of a broader sales development process.

To effectively utilize referrals, it's vital to reach as many decision-makers as possible. As you build your outreach strategy and evaluate relationships with sellers in various accounts, it's important to gain sponsorship to further establish your value within the account. I advocate using referrals strategically in two key parts of the sales process:

- **In the Offer Email:** Towards the end of your email sequence, include a request asking if there is anyone else in the organization who could be relevant to speak with, and whether the current contact could sponsor an introduction. This could be framed as, "Is there someone else in your organization who could also benefit from learning about our solution? Would you be comfortable introducing us?"

- **During the Initial Meeting:** At the conclusion of your first meeting, a simple yet effective question to ask is, "Who else should I be speaking with about this, and if you were in my position, what else should I know?" This not only helps in broadening your network within the company but also deepens your understanding of their needs and internal dynamics.

Incorporating these referral tactics into your sales strategy is essential for penetrating accounts and should be standard practice for enabling sellers to effectively execute your sales strategy.

Use Automation And Digital Selling Technology

As partner sellers utilize their strategic relationships to position solutions, they often need assistance in creating new engagements. In situations where there are no assigned target accounts or strategic partners available for alignment, it is beneficial to assign accounts to partner sellers for Account-Based Marketing strategies. Within the MP3 model, we leverage technologies such as Splashmetrics to standardize and automate the buyer's journey across all outreach efforts. Additionally, tools like Ringdrop.ai offer automated, persona-based outreach capabilities that can be tailored to partner sellers. Integrating these technologies is crucial for enhancing engagement rates and assisting partners in establishing more effective connections.

Figure 34.

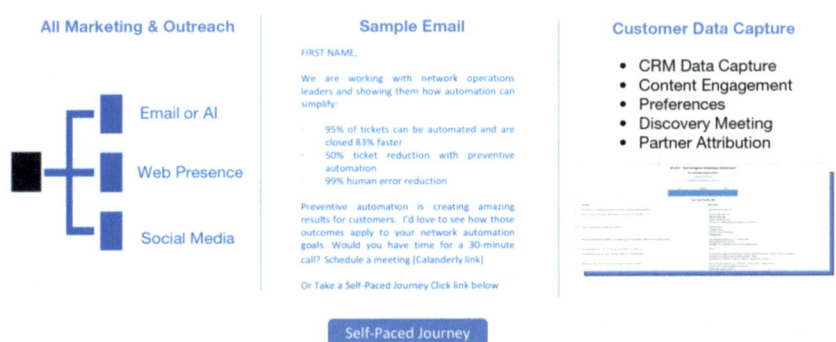

Four: Provide a Qualification Questionnaire

Once the outreach effort culminates in a scheduled meeting with a prospect, it's crucial to ensure that the partner seller is well-prepared, whether the sales approach is co-sell or resale. Partner sellers need to be equipped with a qualification process and a set of specific questions designed to uncover critical information that will help them effectively position your solution according to the customer's buying motivations.

A best practice I advocate is to provide a qualification questionnaire along with your sales play. This questionnaire should be in sync with your company's sales methodology, ensuring that the partner seller asks the same questions your direct seller would. For instance, if the vendor uses the SPIN selling technique, we prepare the partner seller with questions focused on the situation, problem, implication, and need payoff. Similarly, for the MEDDIC approach, the questionnaire would cover Metrics, Economic Buyer, Decision Criteria, Decision Process, Identify Pain, and Champion. This alignment ensures that the partner seller can conduct the meeting as effectively as the vendor's own sales team, fostering consistency in how

140

the solution is presented and enhancing the quality of the meeting to deliver the next step.

Five: Provide a Simple Pitch Deck

While I realize most opportunities are co-sell today with vendors and partners collaborating on sales, it's still important to resource your sales play for a full sales process. One common pitfall in initial meetings is attempting to sell the solution right away. Experienced sales executives know the importance of selling the next step in their sales process instead. This means that the objective of the Discovery meeting isn't to close the deal immediately but to lead the prospect toward the next step in your sales process such as an assessment, a customized demo, a trial, etc.

To keep the meeting focused and effective, it's useful to equip the partner seller with a succinct three-to-five-slide pitch deck. This deck should start by addressing the problem the client is experiencing, followed by how your solution can lead to desirable outcomes, and conclude with a brief overview of how the solution works to achieve these outcomes. The final slide should clearly outline the next step, leading into the validation and proof of value stage.

Note: It's crucial to include training on how to effectively deliver this pitch deck as part of your strategy enablement training for partner sellers. This ensures that they are not only equipped with the right tools but also know how to use them effectively to guide the conversation towards the next critical step in the sales process.

Six: Teach Your Sales Development Process

Co-selling is a significant trend in the channel today, with innovative methodologies from companies like Forecastable addressing the co-sell challenge directly. In co-selling, two distinct companies collaborate to leverage their unique value propositions to engage customers and jointly drive sales. With this approach, it's crucial to align partners within a structured sales development process to ensure both parties can achieve mutually beneficial outcomes.

One best practice is to establish a detailed sales development plan. When I build sales plays, I often provide my clients with a strategy board form that organizes the entire sales development process. This includes stages such as discovery, pre-sales design, relationship mapping, decision-making processes, POV planning, pricing, negotiation leverage, and closure. This structured process is essential to maintain momentum in the co-sell partnership and sales development.

The Strategy Board Form is particularly useful as it clearly outlines potential challenges and the strategies needed to overcome them, explaining how each step will be approached. This tool helps ensure that all involved parties are on the same page and can work together effectively towards closing deals. A sample Strategy Board Form can be seen in Figure 35, offering a visual representation of how these elements come together to support a successful co-sell initiative.

Figure 35.

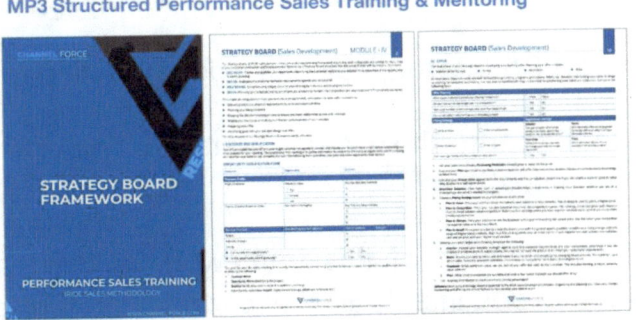

MP3 Structured Performance Sales Training & Mentoring

If you are building a sales play and want access to our Strategy Board Form, reach out to me at info@channel-force.com.

Seven: Link Important Documents

I develop sales plays that follow a structured, logical sequence:

- **Solution Overview:** Explains why the solution should be sold.

- **Sales Metrics and Compensation:** Outlines what's in it for the seller.

- **Targeting Accounts:** Identifies which accounts to target.

- **Value Messaging:** Crafts compelling value propositions.

- **Initial Meeting & Qualification:** Includes the pitch deck and qualification criteria.

- **Deal Registration Process:** Details the steps for registering a deal.

- **Customized Demo Process:** Describes how to tailor demos.

- **Sales Development Process:** Utilizes a strategy board form.

- **Pricing Support:** Provides guidance on pricing strategies.

- **Marketing Collateral:** Includes videos, white papers, etc.

- **How to Expand the Deal:** Strategies for enlarging the scope of a deal.

Ensure each element of this framework is fully resourced. Create links to documents in the partner portal, if available, making it easy for partners to access the information they need.

Your sales play should be a complete recipe with all the necessary ingredients included. If you need a template for a sales play, reach out at info@channel-force.com.

Conclusion

While there are lots of additional details to sales play development, creating effective sales plays demands a thorough comprehension of your sales process and strategy. Generic marketing playbooks fall short in facilitating the necessary knowledge transfer and strategic execution required in today's competitive partner sales landscape. Well-crafted, solution-based sales plays address various channel challenges including revenue generation, relevance, enablement, execution, and return on investment.

Integrating a robust target account mapping process with a compelling sales play forms the core of our structured performance production line. By investing in the development of meticulously thought-out and compelling strategies for sales creation, you position yourself on a trajectory toward doubling your revenue. This approach not only optimizes sales processes but also enhances partner engagement and effectiveness, crucial for achieving significant growth in today's market.

Chapter Application

The MP3 process is specifically designed to address and bridge the skill gaps of partner sellers while amplifying the outcomes produced by your sales strategy and execution. This isn't to suggest that partner sellers are less skilled than vendors; rather, partner sellers often have a broader array of solutions to offer and typically cannot specialize to the same extent in any one product.

To ensure precise execution, MP3 introduces sales plays that provide a clear, step-by-step guide for partner sellers to follow. Like any endeavor in life, the quality of your sales plays and the depth of your enablement efforts will directly impact the performance and productivity of the seller.

The goal for this chapter was to provide a few best practices for developing high-performance sales plays that not only engage but actively transform passive sellers into proactive prospectors. I hope you gain value from some of the foundational techniques I employ to develop sophisticated messaging that not only activates sellers but also compels economic buyers to take action.

Building High-Performance Sales Plays

To craft effective sales plays that support the buyer's journey and deliver compelling messaging, it is essential to:

One: Take Inventory of Your Solution Sales Process: Start with a blueprint that identifies market opportunities and outlines a tested sales process to effectively capture these opportunities. Our methodology treats sales plays like a recipe, providing clear instructions and guidelines necessary for systematic execution.

Two: Align Sales your Strategies with Buyer Personas: Develop detailed customer profiles and tailor value propositions to meet the specific needs and expectations of different segments, ensuring the messaging resonates and addresses the priority problems of each persona.

Three: Map Out the Buyer's Journey: Detail the stages of the buyer's journey—from awareness through decision-making—and align your sales strategies to effectively guide potential customers towards making a purchase.

By adhering to these practices, you ensure your sales plays are not only strategically sound but also practically executable, significantly enhancing your ability to generate active sellers and inspire economic buyers effectively. This structured approach is pivotal in transforming your sales process into a high-performance engine, driving substantial revenue growth.

MP3-PERFORMANCE MANAGEMENT (OUTPUTS)

9

In the early 1980s, the Theory of Constraints (TOC) was introduced to address the challenges faced by organizations in achieving their goals and optimizing their performance. Dr. Eliyahu M. Goldratt developed TOC in response to the prevalent inefficiencies and constraints observed in various production systems. Traditional management approaches focused on optimizing individual parts of a system without considering their interconnectedness, leading to suboptimal overall performance. TOC was designed to provide a systematic framework for identifying and managing constraints—factors that limit an organization's ability to achieve its objectives. By focusing on constraints and implementing strategies to address them effectively, TOC aims to improve efficiency, productivity, and overall success in organizations across different sectors.

Without monitoring and control systems in place, every production line loses efficiency. The need for performance intelligence is essential to manage production processes to achieve optimal performance. The same holds true for partner-powered sales performance. What metrics can we collect to tell us the health of our partner ecosystem sales acceleration process? What constraints do I need to focus on to improve the productivity of my partner ecosystem? This is the challenge of the program-centric partnering model, no system controls.

Conventional channel analytics offer a narrow perspective, primarily relying on historical data such as Point of Sale (POS), Forecasts and Program Compliance metrics. While these metrics are valuable, they only provide a retrospective snapshot of past performance or a subjective view of future performance without delving into the underlying reasons. As a result, channel leaders are left to conjecture about the factors driving trends and performance patterns. In essence, today's prevailing partnering metrics lack the depth needed to offer visibility and control to manage the efficiency of the partner ecosystem's sales performance.

In our pursuit of profitable and efficient revenue growth, through the development of a partner-powered revenue engine, it's imperative to establish robust system controls capable of swiftly identifying and resolving issues. This chapter explores the current landscape of channel analytics and introduces strategy execution visibility as the next evolution in partner management. Strategy execution visibility addresses the absence of crucial system control elements in today's partner analytics. This innovative approach is crucial to enhance partner sales performance in today's complex partnering environment. The MP3 process and our associated tools are designed to bridge the visibility gap in executing sales creation strategies. Our novel ChannelOps math equation provides a comprehensive overview of the channel sales process by integrating traditional partner performance metrics with strategy execution metrics. This holistic perspective is instrumental to comprehend and enhance the effectiveness of your sales channels.

Current Channel Analytics

In many channel organizations, the prevailing analytics model separates data into two main categories:

- **Sales Metrics:** Which includes the historical point of sales and forecast data.

■ **Program Performance:** Which tracks program compliance achievements.

While these traditional metrics offer insights into past sales achievements and help with forecasting future performance, they frequently fail to explain the underlying reasons for these outcomes. This is precisely where strategy execution visibility becomes essential, as it fills the crucial gap in understanding the "Why?" behind the numbers. Consider the performance data currently collected in channel operations. Much of it is circumstantial and not immediately actionable. Typically, this data offers a retrospective snapshot, acting as an inspection point for actions taken months later. For instance, Point of Sale (POS) data only reveals what partners achieved in the previous quarter. Now, imagine the impact on your revenue if you had weekly insights into strategy execution data that was immediately actionable, clearly defining the health of your pipeline production line. This is the strength of a data-driven performance model that operates at both the seller and account levels!

This strategy execution visibility goes beyond tracking opportunistic channel performance by providing structured, real-time insights into how partners are executing the joint sales strategy. This involves gathering data on partner prospecting activities, marketing initiatives, market development efforts, sales play implementation, and metrics related to opportunity development. Collecting this data is crucial for understanding the dynamics behind certain trends and pinpointing the reasons for their occurrence.

Incorporating strategy execution metrics into contemporary channel analytics introduces precise measurement and accountability into the target account mapping process. For partner leaders, capturing this data is essential for monitoring partner progress in developing pipelines for new business. It establishes accountability by documenting partner seller execution and enables the segmentation of reports by sales play, channel manager, partner, and account. Developing ChannelOps dashboards provides a solid framework for accountability, offering significant benefits to all parties involved:

- **Partners:** Enhance sales efficiencies by monitoring the performance of their account managers and sales engineers in securing high-margin new sales.

- **Channel Managers:** Profit from a structured process that incorporates measurement and accountability for active seller and account engagement trending. These ChannelOps dashboards provide the performance intelligence to help transform the partner community from fulfilling orders to actively developing sales. Which leads to greater revenue, quota attainment, and commission.

- **Sales Teams:** Gain advantages from insights on partner prospecting activities and enhanced account coverage by active partner sellers, leading to new sales generation. Structured coverage accelerates time-to-revenue, resulting in greater sales volume, higher quota attainment, and increased commissions.

Strategy execution intelligence allows you to answer critical questions such as "Is the partner creating sales value?" and "Who are my top-performing partner sellers?" Transitioning partner performance metrics from traditional measures like program compliance, point of sale, and forecast data to strategy execution and partner seller activity offers a clearer view of the partner's strength and the effectiveness of our channel sales strategy. This shift enables you to cut through the metaphorical fog by merging POS/CRM data with partner strategy execution insights, presenting a comprehensive view of past, current, and future ecosystem performance on a single CRM dashboard. Our new ChannelOps math equation and MP3 performance management system capture and display key metrics like active seller prospecting activity in near real-time. See Figure 36 for a visual representation.

Figure 36.

New Channel Math

New Market Target Engagement Rate 18%	Growth Market Target Engagement Rate 22%	Mature Market Target Engagement Rate 10%	Decline Target Engagement Rate 5%

Active Sellers	Coverage	Engagement Rate	Engagements	Conversion Rate	Deal Size	New Funnel Value
40	160	22%	35	30%	$150K	$1.575M
Four Target Accounts Each.	Active Target Accounts	Based On Market Dynamics	Generated By Sales Play & TAP	Meetings to Opportunities (Deal Registration)	Average	30% of 35 = 10.5 10.5 x $150K

Note:
- Active Sellers= Enabled and actively Prospect in 4 Target Accounts or 4 Economic Buyer's
- Coverage= Total accounts Active Sellers are Prospecting in for the quarter.
- Engagement Rates= Meetings / By number of Accounts Targeted.
- Conversion Rate= Meetings that have progressed to a quote sent to the customer.
- Benchmarking (Goals + Performance)

How MP3 Performance Management Works!

In our MP3 performance management framework, we significantly redefine the role of the Partner Account Manager. Instead of just overseeing a roster of partners, they now actively develop and manage a network of engaged individual sellers. This strategic shift is crucial for encouraging proactive sales activities targeted at specific accounts, facilitating a dynamic and measurable approach to sales across different dimensions, such as sales plays, partner account managers, and individual accounts.

At the heart of our performance management methodology is the consistent weekly tracking of the 4-3-2-1 prospecting activities. Tracking prospecting activity plays a critical role in capturing essential performance indicators, including the number of active sellers, number of accounts covered, engagement rate percentage, number of meetings held, conversion rates, and average deal size. These metrics form a clear framework for evaluating and steering performance.

This new approach offers a transformative way to manage performance within the channel. By focusing on prospecting metrics, you not only gain a clearer understanding of the effectiveness of your sales activities but also establish a system that naturally encourages and rewards productive and strategic sales behaviors. This shift in performance management, from a partner-focused (factory level) approach to one centered on active selling and strategic engagement (production line), promises a more robust and results-oriented partner ecosystem.

Performance Management With New Math

The MP3 ChannelOps dashboard revolutionizes the management of partner sales by providing deep insights through trend analysis on crucial performance indicators. This powerful tool equips leaders with the ability to delve into previously elusive data, offering a detailed view of their channel's dynamics and efficacy. With MP3, leaders can thoroughly assess various aspects of their operations, such as:

■ **Active Partner Sellers:** Total number, breakdown per partner, and per Channel Account Manager (CAM).

■ **Account Coverage:** Details on which accounts are covered and the scope of that coverage.

■ **Targeted Prospecting:** Identification of targeted entities and the specific prospecting activities executed at the role or account level.

- **Outreach Outcomes:** Results of each outreach effort, including emails, calls, and referrals.

- **Sales Play Effectiveness:** Analysis of how many meetings each sales play has generated, participant involvement, and scheduling.

- **Conversion Rates:** Conversion metrics from meetings to the sales funnel, including deal registrations.

- **Deal Size and Close Rate:** Examination of average deal size and the success rates of closures.

- **Individual Partner Performance:** Performance metrics for each partner concerning their sales and engagement activities.

- **CAM Performance:** Evaluation of how each CAM is managing and driving partner activities and overall sales.

- **Trend Analysis:** Comprehensive month-over-month (MoM) and year-over-year (YoY) trends across these metrics.

Our detailed, data-driven approach allows leaders to make informed decisions and strategically steer their partner sales initiatives.

The MP3 ChannelOps dashboard transforms channel sales management by granting leaders access to an unprecedented depth and breadth of data. This tool does more than just display data—it allows leaders to thoroughly analyze and comprehend the effectiveness of their strategies and the productivity of their teams. With this enhanced understanding, leaders are empowered to make more informed decisions, leading to improved sales performance and better strategic outcomes.

Using MP3 Dashboards to Diagnose Issues

The MP3 ChannelOps dashboard revolutionizes the way ecosystem performance and potential issues are identified and addressed, starting from the analysis of active sellers. It offers a comprehensive trending analysis on the number of active partner sellers (sales reps), providing a clear picture of the partner community's salesforce engagement level over time. The dashboard further breaks down the performance into several key areas:

- **Coverage:** This metric shows the number of target accounts assigned, giving a clear view of the market reach.

- **Engagement Rates:** Defined as the percentage of meetings generated relative to the targeted accounts, this metric offers insight into how effectively sellers are engaging with potential clients.

- **Total Engagements:** Represents the aggregate number of meetings held, providing a snapshot of overall seller activity.

- **Conversion Rates:** This critical metric indicates the proportion of meetings that have progressed to a quoted opportunity, highlighting the effectiveness of sales pitches and client interactions.

- **Average Deal Size:** Calculated as the total quoted dollar amount divided by the number of opportunities, this figure helps in understanding the value potential of each opportunity.

Uniquely, each of these elements can be sorted by sales play, partner, and CAM, and filtered by date for detailed trending analysis. This granularity enables partner leaders to pinpoint specific areas for improvement and set targeted Key Performance Indicators (KPIs).

For instance, a downward trend in active sellers prompts an inspection point to correct the issue. Similarly, high engagement rates coupled with low conversion rates signal a need for improvement in the discovery meeting and deal development phases. These insights are crucial for fine-tuning strategies and enhancing overall sales effectiveness.

In essence, the MP3 ChannelOps dashboard offers actionable data that channel leaders have never had access to before. It's not just a tool for viewing data but an instrument for deep analysis, enabling leaders to make informed decisions and strategic adjustments in real-time, based on concrete performance metrics.

Insights Are Only As Good As The Data Inputs

The MP3 ChannelOps dashboard is a groundbreaking tool for channel management, but its effectiveness depends on the quality of the data inputs. In our approach, sales plays are created within the Performance IQ tool. Each sales play is assigned specific outreaches to target accounts and economic buyers. Partners and partner sellers are also mapped to these outreaches. The MP3 process follows a specific sequence to implement the 4-3-2-1 prospecting method, requiring active partner sellers to regularly provide data to the vendor account owner or partner manager. The quality of the data provided impacts the quality of the ChannelOps dashboard. Here are some best practices to ensure data quality.

Best Practices: To ensure robust vendor-partner seller engagement and the accuracy of data inputs, here are some best practices:

- **Pay for Data:** While it might seem unconventional, it's common for companies to purchase data. I suggest that vendors incorporate a data engagement incentive into their deal registration process. By providing additional margin opportunities in exchange for detailed 4-3-2-1 prospecting activity data, vendors effectively incentivize and 'pay' for high-quality data. This approach turns data submission into a mutually beneficial arrangement.

- **Vendor Sales Leadership Buy-In:** It's crucial for vendor sales leadership to commit to managing their teams for data accuracy. When partner sellers submit their weekly data, having the Channel Account Manager (CAM) copied on these interactions serves as a secondary verification method. Additionally, integrating the MP3 dashboard into weekly forecast calls reinforces its importance and utility.

- **Incentivize Initial Data Submission:** Offering incentives for submitting data during the initial engagements can encourage timely and accurate data entry.

- **Educate on the Benefits:** Convincing partner sellers of the value that data brings is key. Explain how their contributions help in creating more effective sales plays and engagements, ultimately leading to higher win rates and mutual benefits.

While no system is flawless, these best practices lay the groundwork for ensuring data accuracy and enhancing overall performance. The MP3 dashboard, when fueled by accurate and timely data, becomes an invaluable asset for channel strategy execution and management.

Note: Requesting 4-3-2-1 prospecting activity updates from partner sellers can be challenging, as no one likes to feel micromanaged, especially by a vendor. When I designed the MP3 process, the intention was never to manage partner sellers. Instead, the data is used to identify issues and build better sales plays and messaging to help sellers improve engagement, conversion, and close rates. For example, by tracking outreaches, we can see when meetings are generated. If the messaging from the first email rarely creates a meeting, we want to know so we can adjust the messaging to find what works. It's important to remember that active sellers are volunteers who can opt in or out of the process at any time. The data we request benefits all sellers, aiming to create profitable, efficient time-to-value at the seller level.

Automation Versus Data Input

You have probably picked up on the fact that MP3 is not an automated process at the moment. The entire world is moving towards automation and AI-driven data collection and insights to ensure accuracy and reduce the administrative burden of data collection. While this trend is promising and will eventually become an option in the MP3 Planning and Performance IQ toolset, our model intentionally encourages co-sell engagements between partner sellers, vendor sellers, and Partner Account Managers. We aim for weekly interactions to share insights, build relationships, and foster trust. Data collection is an integral part of these engagements, providing a reason to connect.

Chapter Application

I recognize that much of this Chapter is proprietary to implementing the MP3 process. However, even if you don't use our methodology, the principles of measuring and managing active sellers will apply to your channel process. I encourage CROs, Partner Pros, and RevOps to complement their partner-level metrics with active seller metrics to better understand the strategy execution performance of your partner ecosystem.

The MP3 ChannelOps math equation helps you make the shift and revolutionizes partner performance analytics. This formula helps revenue leaders bridge the visibility gap inherent in today's opportunistic channel models. By utilizing this straightforward ChannelOps math equation, you can clearly demonstrate the value of your partnership programs.

In addition, MP3 enhances visibility across the entire sales creation process—from strategy and execution to partners, sellers, channel managers, and accounts. This detailed approach gives you a method to manage strategy execution that has previously been lacking. Employing the ChannelOps math equation, leaders can now run the partner ecosystem as efficiently as a production line.

This method allows for the evaluation of monthly input performance, including the number of active sellers and target accounts, as well as production line efficiency metrics like engagement rates, conversion rates, and average deal size. Outputs such as total new pipeline can be quantified. Trend analysis on each of these elements enables leaders to inspect trends, devise new strategies, and set KPIs to either reinforce successes or correct course. This ChannelOps dashboard provides CROs with the metrics they need to position the value of the channel with their board!

The MP3 data-driven, structured performance partnering model marks a significant change from the traditional, less predictable "partner and pray" models. Now, we can manage inputs to ensure desired outputs, harnessing the power of data to drive strategic decisions in the partner sales creation process.

Note: Channel Force Inc. offers Performance IQ, our performance intelligence application in both a Salesforce version or for small deployments a Google version. This tool allows for account mapping and captures the prospecting activities of partner sellers. It delivers comprehensive dashboards and trend analyses by sales play, partner, and channel account manager. To discover how Performance IQ can enhance your sales strategy, visit www.channel-force.com and schedule a meeting to learn more.

10

TERRITORY MANAGEMENT

Channel Territory Management has traditionally centered on the art of managing partner relationships, emphasizing joint business strategies, partner engagements, partner program compliance, sales enablement, and revenue per partner. However, as the focus shifts to measuring value through the lens of profitable and efficient revenue growth, a transformation is underway. Progressive revenue leaders seeking better visibility, control, and predictability of their ecosystem revenue production process are prioritizing the management of active sellers and target account coverage. This chapter explores this transformation, illustrating how the MP3 partner-powered sales acceleration model adapts to these changes, particularly through the innovative 5-4-2 Territory Management Principle.

Partner Management vs. Active Seller Focus

Traditionally, partner account management emphasized the breadth of relationships. Partner Managers were tasked with overseeing numerous partnerships and ensuring overall satisfaction without a direct focus on individual seller sales productivity. This approach, while comprehensive, often lacked a mechanism to drive consistent sales outcomes.

Contrastingly, Channel Force's shift to managing active sellers within a territory introduces a focused, quantitative approach to channel management. In the MP3 process, a partner account manager's role is redefined to creating and managing 40 "active sellers" each quarter. An active seller is defined as a partner seller that is proactively engaged with four targeted accounts or economic buyers, executing the 4-3-2-1 prospecting process. This strategic shift ensures that every active seller acts as a unit of production for the quarter, directly contributing to the sales output of the territory.

Figure 37.

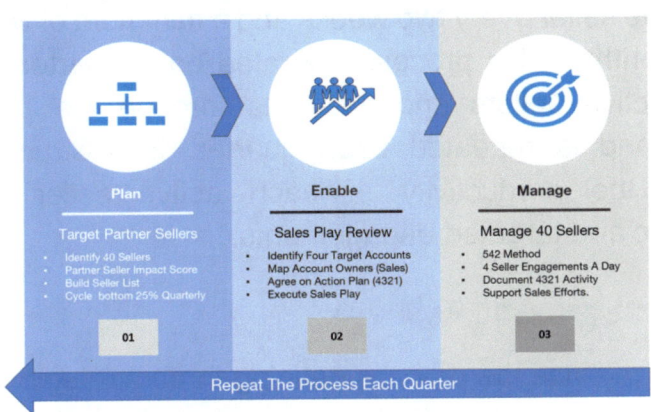

Simple Active Sellers Management Process

Transitioning territory management from partnerships to active sellers represents a significant shift in priorities, necessitating a structured approach to ensure optimal performance. From a production line perspective, partner managers ensure the production process maintains the necessary level of activity to meet our output goal, the partner revenue target. This entails the partner manager's monitoring and providing support at the production line level to active sellers.

Channel Force Inc. has devised a streamlined process known as 5-4-2, which is pivotal in optimizing this new focus. At the heart of this approach lies the 5-4-2 Management Process, designed to efficiently handle 40 active sellers. 5-4-2 stands for:

- 5 Days a week.

- 4 Seller engagements a day.

- 2 Direct connects each month.

Partner Managers strategically organize their weeks to engage with 20 active sellers per week, ensuring direct contact with each active seller every two weeks and a minimum of two touch points monthly. This process operates on a quarterly basis, cycling active sellers and accounts through the pipelining process and is repeated each quarter. It is structured to enhance the productivity of each active seller through systematic and targeted engagements.

The Management Process

Figure 37 outlines the process defining three strategic steps:

One: **Sales Play Enablement:** This initial step involves educating partner sellers on your sales play and execution strategy. The enablement sessions are designed to align the sellers' efforts with a defined market opportunity and position the incentives to create proactive prospecting behaviors.

Note: Partnerships can have multiple sales plays running simultaneously. However, at the seller level, I recommend focusing on one sales play per seller, which can be cycled each quarter.

Two: **Target Account Mapping:** Following enablement, the next step is to score potential accounts based on an Ideal Customer Profile and the Relationship Score of the active seller with the targeted economic buyer. This mapping ensures that efforts are concentrated on the most promising opportunities, thereby maximizing the chances of conversion.

Note: The sales play enablement, target account mapping, and account assignment process follows a 90-day cycle per active seller. Ideally, you will enable sellers during the initial four weeks of each quarter, but enablement and account mapping will be ongoing monthly activities. Activating 40 active sellers each quarter takes time, and you may fall short in the first 2-3 quarters. However, over time, you will build a stable of reliable sellers who consistently produce results.

Three: Daily Engagement Routines: The daily management of "active sellers" is structured around making four connections each day to monitor progress and address any challenges in prospecting. These connections could be via emails or direct calls. Importantly, there is a requirement for at least two direct conversations each month with each active seller to ensure fidelity to the prospecting process.

Note: These engagements serve a crucial purpose by capturing 4-3-2-1 prospecting progress and helping align support to address issues with engagements, messaging, meeting preparation, deal development, and more. Consistent engagements help establish your brand and keep sellers on track to deliver results.

Streamlining Sales through Active Engagement

The regular interactions under the 5-4-2 Management Principle not only keep the sales team aligned with strategic goals but also foster a proactive environment where challenges are addressed swiftly and effectively. This active management style is crucial in maintaining high engagement levels among partner sellers, ensuring they feel supported and are more likely to achieve their sales targets.

Benefits of Active Seller Management

The 5-4-2 Management Process offers several compelling benefits that mark a significant departure from traditional channel management:

- **Increased Productivity:** By focusing on a set number of active sellers, the partner manager can more effectively allocate resources and support, leading to higher productivity per seller.

- **Enhanced Accountability:** The regular check-ins and structured engagement process ensure that each active seller remains accountable to their targets, driving a more disciplined approach to sales.

- **Scalability:** This approach allows for scalable management practices as each territory can be adjusted based on the productivity of Active Sellers, making it easier to replicate success across different regions.

- **Improved Sales Outcomes:** With a clear focus on targeted accounts and consistent seller engagement, the likelihood of achieving and exceeding sales targets is greatly increased.

Weekly Reporting

Measure, Measure, Measure! This is the new reality for many technology sales professionals! Effective sales leaders understand this challenge and strive to find a healthy balance between administrative duties and empowering sales professionals to take ownership of their roles. Excessive micromanagement and scrutiny can be counterproductive. So, what should channel sales professionals measure and manage to ensure they are effectively executing their sales strategy? Figure 38 outlines four key MP3 metrics:

One: **Sales Enablement Activity:** This involves tracking significant partner enablement activities that help map accounts with our direct sales teams, specifically measuring account mappings by solution and sales play.

Two: **Account Engagement Activity**: How many accounts are active sellers prospecting in.

Three: **Deal Registrations:** These should naturally follow from proactive prospecting by partners. Essentially, deal registrations should stem directly from the preceding enablement activities.

Four: **Quarterly Revenue:** Monitoring progress towards the quarterly revenue target on a weekly basis is crucial. Ideally, channel sales revenue should result directly from the concerted efforts in sales enablement and deal registration.

Figure 38.

Weekly Reporting Active Seller Example

Team Calls Track Weekly Progress, Trending & Performance Issues

To keep things straightforward, I use a simple tracking system in my weekly calls with channel managers. Each manager is expected to provide updates on these four metrics. The tracker offers a snapshot of each territory's activities and how well they align with proactive prospecting efforts. We set quarterly KPIs for each metric and use a color-coding system to visualize progress: black for on target, green for achieved, yellow for jeopardy, and red for failing to meet. This tracker not only highlights progress but also creates a clear visual representation of where each territory stands in relation to its goals. If you are using the Performance IQ software, these reports are created using the ChannelOps dashboard.

Additionally, I ask channel managers to provide leadership answers to three key questions in their weekly updates:

1. What else should I know?
2. What do you need from me or the company to help you succeed?
3. What best practice do you want to share with the team?

The answers to these questions create a priority list to address each week. Good leaders help their teammates succeed. Spend time tackling the list and provide updates on your progress each week. While I recognize that channel sales and channel administration can be more complicated than the elements I track, keeping it simple, empowering people to do their jobs and take ownership of the results, is a great way to lessen their administrative burden. I am a firm believer that we should measure what really matters.

Refining Your Enablement Pitch Best Practice

As you look to turn up active sellers, your enablement pitch is just as important as the sales play and strategy execution training. Here is a crazy story and a set of principles I teach to help partner managers deliver impactful enablement sessions.

Let's start with a crazy sales enablement opening delivered 25 years ago by a Channel Manager that captures the elements of an impactful sales enablement pitch. Here is how this Channel Manager opened our enablement session:

"My product sucks and your customers are going to buy it!" "Give me your attention for the next 30 minutes and I will explain why. In addition, I am going to define three unmatched benefits of our solution, share two use cases that always sell, and position three benefits to you for selling the solution!" "Finally, I will spend the last 10 minutes teaching you how to master selling our solution showing you how to close a $40K margin opportunity every time we engage together with 4 economic buyers that meet our customer profile." "Enablement is a participation sport, so I will pause between transitions to answer questions!"

This was the opening for a sales enablement presentation that still resonates today! What made this enablement session so powerful? Was it just the sensational opening? That was definitely part of the success equation for sure, but there was more to the opening that makes this a great blueprint for sales enablement presentations.

Before we dissect the elements of an impactful enablement presentation, I want to be clear that I am not telling you to start your enablement sessions with "My product sucks!" but there was a reason this Channel Manger started his enablement training that way. The product he was pitching had a reputation for consuming vast amounts of power, overheating and eventually failing. His dramatic opening line was used to defuse the audience, taking a major objection off the table and at the same time capturing everyone's attention. This Channel Manager understood the power of knowing his audience and tailored his delivery for maximum effectiveness.

So what can we learn from this simple and effective opening? Let's identify seven principles our Channel Manager used in his opening statement that will help you deliver an impactful sales enablement opening.

Principle 1. Know your Audience

Tailor your message to capture the attention of your audience. While this may seem obvious, it's easy to get caught up in what is important to us and forget about what's important for our audience to know. What seems important to me may not be important to our audience. It's often a matter of perspective. One best practice is to discuss beforehand with your Partner who will be attending and what's important to cover to make the presentation meaningful.

Principle 2. Frame your Presentation

The Channel Manager told the audience that he needed 30 minutes of their undivided attention. He kept the presentation portion to 20 minutes knowing that the average attention span for a presentation is estimated to be between 5-10 minutes. The Channel Manager was able to stretch the attention span of the audience by covering the agenda in the opening statement telling them how long they needed to stay engaged.

Principle 3. Tell What you're Going to Tell Them

Our Channel Manager defined the agenda and told his audience what to expect in the 30 minutes he would be presenting to include:

1. Why customers will buy.

2. Three unmatched benefits of our solution.

3. Sharing two use cases that always sell.

4. Defining three benefits for you to prioritize selling the solution.

5. Teaching you to master selling the solution and make $40K in margin.

Principle 4. Why Should My Audience Care

Explain the payoff in your opening. Our Channel Manager alluded to several payoffs in his opening to include the benefits of selling the solution and teaching how to master positioning the solution to generate new sales. Communicating what's in it for the audience helps them to stay engaged and focus their attention knowing a payoff is coming. Presentation openings should always address why the audience should care.

Principle 5. Encourage Audience Participation

Our Channel Manager encouraged questions. This is a great way to keep people engaged, as well as gauge how well the presentation is connecting with the audience. Skilled presenters pick up on participation queues and learn to weave those insights into their presentations to connect better with the audience. Be sure to not allow the presentation flow to suffer from too many questions.

Principle 6. Enable the Strategy

Our Channel Manager's pitch was about how to sell the solution including use cases, and benefits to both the customer and the partner. The focus was on product positioning, selling benefits and making it easier for the partner to sell. Creating a good balance between product enablement and sales strategy enablement is key to equipping your partners to generate new demand. Be sure to balance your product and use-case overview with strategy and execution enablement.

Principle 7. Always Use a Call to Action

Your presentation should lead to an action. I heard a statistic from a radio ad the other day that stated "64% of salespeople never ask for the business." That's a crazy statistic since sales pitches are designed to lead a customer to a closing point. Enablement presentations should do the same. Your presentation is nothing more than a setup for your call to action. Including a call to action creates a next step in your partner enablement process and provides a means for measurement and accountability towards your presentation goal.

Understanding the elements of an effective sales enablement pitch is essential to create impactful presentations. Incorporate these simple best practices into your partner sales enablement sessions and you will create meaningful and memorable presentations that hit the mark!

Note: Create a simple Elevator Pitch when talking to potential active sellers. Here is a simple example: "Would you give me 10 minutes of your time, 3 days a week for 3 weeks, if I could *show you how to create and close a $40K margin deal?"* Don't sell your solution, sell what's in it for them!

Chapter Application

Channel Territory Management has traditionally revolved around managing partner relationships broadly across various channels without stringent productivity measures. However, with evolving market demands and the need for greater efficiency, a refined approach is now prioritized, focusing on managing active sellers within territories. This chapter delves into this transformation, highlighting the adaptation of the MP3 Partner Led Sales Acceleration model through the innovative 5-4-2 Territory Management Principle.

Traditionally, partner management emphasized the breadth of relationships rather than the depth, with managers overseeing numerous partners without a direct focus on individual sales productivity. This approach often lacked mechanisms to drive consistent sales outcomes. In contrast, the modern approach focuses on managing active sellers within a territory, introducing a focused, quantitative strategy to channel management. In the MP3 process, a partner account manager's role is redefined to focus on creating and managing "Active Sellers"—partners who engage proactively with multiple accounts using the 4-3-2-1 prospecting process, ensuring each seller directly contributes to the sales output of the territory.

Transitioning from broad partnership management to focusing on active sellers necessitates a structured approach to ensure performance. Adopting a production line perspective, partner managers monitor and support the 'production line'—the active sellers—to meet the partner revenue target. Channel Force Inc. employs a simplified 5-4-2 Management Process to optimize this new focus, organizing weekly engagements to ensure every active seller is contacted bi-weekly, with at least two touch points per month. This cycle of engagement is designed to boost the productivity of each active seller through systematic and targeted interactions.

The benefits of this Active Seller Management via the 5-4-2 process are significant:

- **Increased Productivity:** Focusing on a set number of active sellers allows partner managers to allocate resources more effectively, enhancing productivity per seller.

- **Enhanced Accountability:** Regular check-ins and a structured engagement process ensure active sellers remain committed to their targets, promoting a disciplined sales approach.

- **Scalability:** This approach allows for scalable management practices, making it easier to replicate success across different regions.

- **Improved Sales Outcomes:** With targeted account focus and consistent seller engagement, the likelihood of meeting and exceeding sales targets increases.

To manage this effectively, a simple tracking system is used in weekly calls with channel managers, focusing on key MP3 metrics like Sales Enablement Activity, Account Engagement Activity, Deal Registrations, and Quarterly Revenue. This system, visualized through a color-coded tracker, provides a clear overview of each territory's progress and aligns efforts toward proactive prospecting.

The MP3 Partner-Powered Sales Acceleration model, particularly through the 5-4-2 Territory Management Principle, represents a paradigm shift in channel management, aligning modern sales strategies with dynamic market requirements and driving significant improvements in channel productivity and sales outcomes.

As you implement the 5-4-2 process, you will establish a rhythm that enhances seller engagements, making the process a natural progression that ensures consistent communication. If sellers become unresponsive, it's important to cycle them out and bring in new sellers. The primary role of every partner manager should be to cultivate active sellers. Partner managers should continually seek new partner sellers to enable, maintaining a proactive approach to building and sustaining seller engagement.

As you explore structured performance models, it's important to address several key questions that will provide a comprehensive view of the model and enhance your understanding of its mechanisms. Here are a few additional points to consider and discuss.

Are Ecosystems The Answer?

Over recent years, ecosystems have been touted as the solution to the revenue creation challenges faced by the channel. This concept involves assembling a group of partners, each contributing their expertise and solutions to co-innovate and tackle customer problems. I am a strong proponent of this approach and see genuine value in the co-sell and co-innovation opportunities that ecosystems introduce to the partnering model. However, ecosystem models can significantly benefit from adding a structured performance element.

Consider the power of an ecosystem model with proactive sellers who prospect in a structured fashion with specific territory coverage objectives. Additionally, think about defining your partner types and ecosystem strategy, establishing metrics to be achieved, creating a market coverage model, and resourcing a prospecting strategy tailored to each partner type. This approach allows companies to systematically leverage each partner's reach to the target market to generate leads for each co-innovated solution and the corresponding ecosystem partner.

This is where integrating a structured performance model with an ecosystem strategy creates a winning combination for all parties involved. The channel organization gains the performance metrics and strategy execution visibility needed to achieve better results. Partners benefit from delivering their solutions within the structured ecosystem framework, and customers receive proactive engagement along with innovative solutions tailored to their specific needs. This holistic approach enhances value for every stakeholder, ensuring a more effective and collaborative partnership environment. Figure 39 provides the pros and cons of each model.

Figure 39.

Partner Model Pros and Cons

Partner Model Evolutions		
Fulfillment	**Ecosystems/Platforms**	**Structured Partner Performance**
Pros	**Pros**	**Pros**
• Low Investment Cost • Fast Time to Market • Increased Coverage • Performance Based Incentives	• Flexible (Co-Innovation) • Broader Coverage • Community Centric • Innovation Speed To Market • Consumer Oriented	• Improves Revenue & Channel ROI • Improves Partner Win Rates • Creates Active Sellers • Creates Better Market Coverage • Structures Sales Creation • Strategy Enablement Focused • Provides Execution Visibility • Aligns PAM Function to Sales • Creates Better Sales Engagement • Ecosystem Friendly
Cons	**Cons**	
• Limited Sales Process Control • Flexibility Challenged (SaaS) • Fulfillment Focused Model • Product Centric • Opportunistic • Limited Partner Execution Visibility	• Still Opportunistic Sales • No Structured Demand Creation • Enablement Challenged • New Model Fog • Account Alignment Challenged	**Cons** • Investment in Tools and Training • Adapting & Maintaining Behaviors

While ecosystems offer many benefits, such as flexible consumption, co-innovation, and reduced sales costs, they don't fully address efficiency due to their continued reliance on unstructured go-to-market practices. The next wave of ecosystem innovation must focus on adopting a structured, revenue performance model that aligns closely with strategic objectives for profitable efficient growth. Companies must prioritize strategy enablement by providing partner sellers with a coverage model and a clear methodology to generate new demand. The real answer to revenue growth lies in combining the reach and co-innovation power of ecosystems with the structured performance of MP3.

Is MP3 Just For Channel and Resell Partners?

Structured performance benefits all types of partners. As companies define their partner programs and go-to-market strategies, the principles of the MP3 model can be adapted for each type of partner:

- **Referral Partners:** Equip them with sales plays that enable them to deliver compelling messaging and effectively map target accounts.

- **Managed Service Providers (MSPs):** Benefit from structured Co-Sell strategies, account mapping, and co-branded sales plays, enhancing their ability to collaborate and generate new sales.

- **Influence Partners:** Provide structured and targeted messaging as part of their social media outreaches, helping them influence decision-makers.

- **Services Partners:** Similar to referral partners, train and equip service partners to run sales plays to upsell new clients, leveraging their existing relationships to introduce more products or services.

Structured performance is crucial for every partner type, clearly defining what you want them to do, how it should be done, and when it needs to be completed. The approach of measuring inputs, production, and outputs is universal and essential for driving efficiency and effectiveness across all types of partnerships.

Is Technology The Answer to Growth?

A recent LinkedIn post highlighted 12 different technology categories within the channel, each featuring over five companies. This showcase of innovation within the partnering model is undoubtedly exciting, as it demonstrates a vibrant effort to enhance how partnerships are managed and optimized. Yet, this diversity also brings to light the potential costs and complexities of managing a tech stack composed of 12 different tools for channel operations.

The primary issue with such a channel tech stack is that it consists mainly of point products, each designed to address specific issues without consideration of a unifying methodology. This can result in what I call a "Frankenstein" approach, where the various solutions do not integrate well, leading to inefficiencies and compatibility issues.

For a channel tech stack to be truly effective, it should seamlessly integrate with the three core technologies that every company relies on: ERP systems, CRM systems, and Martech systems. These integrations are crucial for creating a streamlined, functional, and cohesive technology ecosystem that supports the channel's unique needs without adding undue complexity or disrupting existing processes. By focusing on integrating channel technologies with these foundational systems, companies can avoid the pitfalls of a disjointed tech stack and leverage their existing investments to enhance channel performance.

A robust tech stack is undoubtedly crucial in today's partnering model and can significantly enhance outcomes. However, to truly unlock the sales potential of your partner ecosystem and drive profitable, efficient growth, it is essential to tackle the fundamental challenge of creating active sellers and improving account engagement.

While the potential of Generative AI solutions in the channel is promising, the combination of structured performance and strong, leveraged relationships is likely to yield better results over time. The reason is simple: purchasing decisions are based on trust. People still value relationships and the ability to connect with those they do business with on a social and empathetic level. Current technology, including the tech stack and AI, hasn't fully bridged this gap yet. To maximize effectiveness, we need tools that not only automate and optimize but also enhance and support the human aspects of sales and partnerships. The MP3 Tech stack of Planning and Performance IQ stack is built to integrate into Salesforce CRM systems. For smaller companies, we have a standalone version of our planning software and performance intelligence application.

Do I Need a Partner Portal With MP3?

Partner portals have evolved significantly over the last five years, transforming into a multi-functional tool to accelerate the value of partner programs. Companies like Mindmatrix are revolutionizing these portals by aligning them with methodologies such as MP3. MP3 integrates seamlessly with the partner portal, managing reports, target account mapping workflows, marketing engagement, and much more. While a portal is not strictly necessary to execute MP3, aligning our process with next-generation companies like Mindmatrix will streamline our operations and better organize the partner community.

What are the Challenges with MP3?

Every model has its pros and cons, and the MP3 structured performance model is no exception. Here are some of the challenges associated with implementing MP3:

- **Fundamental Shift in Partnering Approach:** Adopting MP3 requires a significant change in how we approach partnering. Years of experience with the program-centric model have created a kind of "muscle memory." MP3 challenges partner leaders to shift their focus from prioritizing partnerships and programs to balancing these with prioritizing active seller development and prospecting.

- **Changing Role of Partner Account Managers (PAMs):** The MP3 model transforms the role of PAMs. They are required to develop and manage active sellers and administer a comprehensive target account mapping process. This shift may necessitate a different skill set than what has been required under previous models.

- **Data Collection and Management:** The model depends on robust data collection to build revenue roadmaps and manage the sales acceleration process effectively. This shift requires adopting new data collection and management practices, which not every partner may be willing or able to provide.

- **Introduction of New Tools and Training:** Implementing MP3 involves introducing new tools and requires training, which in turn necessitates the development of new policies and processes that must be integrated into existing workflows.

Despite these challenges, solutions are available to address them, and the benefits of implementing MP3 significantly outweigh these obstacles. The structured performance approach enhances strategy execution visibility, improves sales productivity, and ultimately leads to better overall performance across the partner ecosystem.

Note: The future of MP3 is the evolution to a platform with automated data capture to build the planning metrics and performance intelligence elements of our production line process. The platform approach solves the data capture issues automating the MP3 processes.

We Are Doing This Today!

Over the past year, as I've discussed structured performance models with partner leaders, I typically encounter two types of reactions:

1. "Wow, I have never seen anything like this."
2. "We are doing this today."

When leaders claim they are already implementing this model, I probe further to understand their methods. Often, I find that while companies may have high-level sales plays or some form of account mapping, they lack a cohesive methodology that brings everything together. To put it simply, it's like having several car parts in the garage but not knowing how to assemble them into a high-performance vehicle.

If you believe your model is already running a structured performance model, ask yourself the following questions:

1. Does my model indicate the number of active sellers and account engagements required, along with the time frames for achieving these metrics, to meet the revenue goal?

2. Can I detail how many active sellers I have, the accounts they are targeting, and the prospecting activities they are involved in?

3. Can I specify my engagement rates, conversion rates, and close rates by solution?

4. Do I know how many accounts are covered and the strength of relationships with each partner in these accounts?

5. Can I model revenue and resource allocation effectively?

6. Can I predict my revenue based on active sellers and account coverage?

These questions highlight the effectiveness of a structured performance model. The real value for revenue leaders lies in creating a production line process with the precise controls of a factory setting—a capability not commonly found in many partnering models today.

MP3 Seem Too Complicated?

While structured performance models like MP3 do require more administrative effort than traditional program-centric models, they are not as daunting as they might appear. MP3 involves adding revenue planning with only 14 key inputs, structured coverage through target account mapping, and performance intelligence to track account engagement activities. The initial setup may need some training and fine-tuning, but once companies are operating within the MP3 process, many job functions become streamlined, creating operational efficiencies within the partnering organization.

Additionally, there are various ways to integrate MP3 into your existing partnering model. Companies can gradually implement this approach by starting with a "tip of the spear" model as shown in Figure 40, or they can adopt specific parts of the model according to their needs. For instance, some companies may begin with structured coverage and sales plays by adopting the target account planning process, while initially omitting elements like revenue planning or performance intelligence at the backend. This flexibility allows companies to tailor the model and adopt only the components that best suit their needs.

Figure 40.

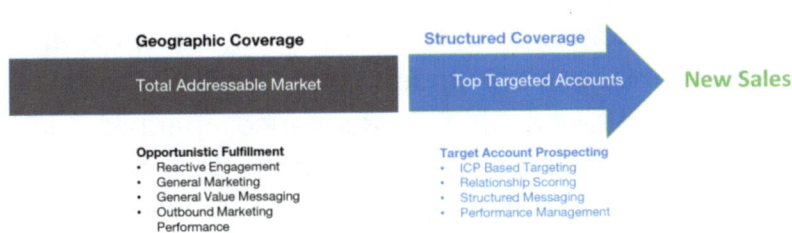

Structured Market Coverage Model

What Is The Ideal Customer Profile For MP3?

Structured performance models can enhance any partnering model, regardless of size. I particularly recommend the MP3 framework for companies that already have a portfolio of existing partners, an established partner program, unstructured go-to-market processes, or are struggling to improve revenue outcomes. Additionally, the pricing model for the Planning and Performance IQ tools is based on the number of Partner Account Managers, making the initial investment low and allowing scalability according to user numbers. This flexible pricing structure ensures that companies can start small and expand as their needs grow.

What Are Some Myths about Partnering?

The biggest challenges to structured performance models come from common partnering myths that oversimplify partnering and create challenges for Partner Pros that know what it takes to build a world-class partnering model these myths include:

One: **Build It And They Will Come:** The first misconception surrounding partner performance revolves around the "build it and they will come" ideology. This oversimplified perspective assumes that merely establishing a partner program, enlisting a few partners, and educating them on the product offerings will automatically generate revenue. However, those experienced in partner management understand this is far from reality. Crafting a thriving, high-performance partner program demands significant investment and a well-thought-out strategy, challenging the notion that success in partnerships is as straightforward as simply setting up the program. A good partnering model considers market awareness, consumer needs, competition, customer engagement, evolving market dynamics, and the necessity of building trust.

Two: **What I Did In The Past Will Work In The Future:** The second fallacy lies in the belief that past methods will guarantee future success. Many companies and Partner leaders place too much emphasis on previous strategies and processes, mistakenly believing that replicating past actions will yield similar outcomes. However, the channel landscape is not immune to change. With the continuous evolution of technology, consumption models, and buying behaviors, it's imperative that our strategies adapt to sustain high performance. This principle extends to personal development too; as revenue leaders, we must embrace adaptation and continuous professional growth to avoid becoming obsolete in a rapidly changing environment. Relying solely on previous successes without adapting to current and future changes leads to stagnation and missed opportunities. Success requires agility, continuous learning, and the willingness to innovate and experiment with new approaches, rather than resting on past laurels.

Three: Activity Equals Results: The third misconception is equating activity with results. As revenue leaders, we often gauge success by the volume of activities undertaken by our teams, individual contributors and partners, under the assumption that more activity directly translates to better outcomes. However, it's not merely about the quantity of activity, but rather the quality and relevance of these actions. Ensuring that your teams and partners are equipped with the right tools and processes to align with your strategic goals is what truly drives results. Simply ticking off tasks leads to superficial outcomes. It's crucial for revenue leaders to identify and measure activities that genuinely contribute to the desired results. The traditional partner model often falls short here, focusing on compliance and forecasting instead of more impactful metrics, like the number of active partner sellers, their prospecting efforts, coverage of target accounts, and actual sales achievements. Shifting the focus to these areas provides the clarity and outcome-oriented approach necessary to demonstrate your value to company leadership.

Four: People Care About Partner Programs: Considerable effort goes into crafting partner programs to streamline processes and ensure fairness within the channel, yet the stark reality is that the intricacies of these programs often go unnoticed. What truly matters is revenue generation and sales performance for your company, ease of sale and market potential for your partners, and how well your solutions meet the urgent needs of your customers. It's time for a paradigm shift in channel strategy, focusing more on fostering the connection between partner sellers and the target market, rather than just between the vendor and the partner. This is not to undermine the value of partner programs; they lay the groundwork for more critical aspects of business. To truly enhance the role of the channel, the focus should shift towards prioritizing sales and leading conversations with sales initiatives rather than the mechanics of partner program objectives.

These misunderstandings underscore the importance of adopting a structured planning process and methodology for crafting effective solution sales strategies that tap into the dynamic sales force within the partner ecosystem.

How Do I Sell MP3 To My CRO?

One of the primary challenges for a Chief Revenue Officer (CRO) is achieving profitable, efficient revenue growth. The partner ecosystem offers a significant opportunity to achieve this. However, a major issue with program-centric partnering models is the disconnect between sales and partnerships, often characterized by differing languages and approaches aimed at achieving the same results. The MP3 framework is the first methodology specifically designed to bridge this gap between partnering and sales. It enhances a company's existing sales methods by utilizing partner-sourced leads to create top-of-funnel co-sell opportunities that can be developed into closed deals. This integration leads to the MP3X model, where "MP3" represents the partnering methodology and "X" the company's current sales methodology, thus allowing MP3 to enhance any sales approach with a robust front-end pipeline process.

Moreover, MP3 equips CROs with the tools to clearly articulate the value of the channel to the board and manage revenue growth through effective performance management of active sellers. This not only streamlines communication but also aligns channel efforts with broader corporate objectives. The MP3 Revenue Planning Tools and ChannelOps Dashboard provide CROs a way to finally articulate the value of the partner program to the board in a clear and concise manner.

IMPLEMENTING CHANGE FOR FUTURE SUCCESS

In the mid-20th century, W. Edwards Deming, a statistician from Iowa, revolutionized production line quality control, altering the global manufacturing landscape. His quality control ideas, developed during the post-war American manufacturing boom, emphasized improving productivity through process refinement, systemic thinking, and statistical methods. Despite initial rejection in the U.S., where leaders favored quantity over quality, Deming's methods focused on continuous improvement in production and management, promoting a collaborative environment between workers and management.

Deming's fortunes changed dramatically when he was invited by Japanese industrial leaders in the 1950s to help revive their war-torn economy. Japanese companies like Toyota and Honda embraced his principles, integrating his statistical process control methods and broader philosophies about quality and productivity into their manufacturing processes. This adoption sparked a quality revolution in Japan, leading to significant improvements in the reliability and performance of Japanese products. By the 1970s and 1980s, Japanese automobiles, which were once ridiculed for their poor quality, began to dominate global markets, surpassing many American manufacturers who had initially dismissed his innovative approaches.

Modern Parallel In Partner Sales Models

Today, the opportunistic partnering model finds itself at a similar inflection point faced by post-war American manufacturers. The current, program-centric channel model is losing effectiveness, relying on measuring activities at the partner level instead of moving downstream to the production line, measuring active sellers and target account engagements. Just as Deming's methodologies revolutionized manufacturing by integrating systemic quality improvements, there is a critical need for partnering models to follow a similar data-driven approach.

The time for change is now. Companies that embrace this new methodology will ignite a partner-powered revenue revolution in their partner ecosystem. Those who fail to adapt risk being outpaced by more agile and innovative partner leaders who understand the evolving market dynamics. Just as American auto manufacturers eventually adopted Deming's processes, today's partnering models will adopt some form of structured performance with ChannelOps math equations.

Why MP3 For Today's Partnering Model?

We began this book by exploring sales methodologies, building the need for a structured performance partnering model. The traditional partner-centric model, built on best-effort unstructured sales principles, is losing effectiveness. There's a revolution taking place in the channel focused on managing sales performance to achieve profitable efficient growth. The MP3 process is distinguished as the first comprehensive, data-driven, structured performance partnering methodology specifically designed to enhance partner-powered revenue growth while reducing costs. Our approach provides a streamlined and effective framework for maximizing revenue efficiency through strategic partner engagements. The MP3 structured performance process revolutionizes the partnering model introducing many key innovations:

- **Revenue Planning:** This allows companies to define the metrics necessary to reach a revenue target and to map the resources needed to achieve the metrics.

- **Active Seller and Account Coverage:** Shifting the focus to active sellers and account coverage significantly transforms the partnering model. This granular focus is essential for detailed planning and enables precise sales production and performance intelligence. Monitoring prospecting and account coverage trends are crucial metrics for managing pipeline creation.

- **Structured Prospecting:** Establishing a standard process for managing active seller productivity and scalability. The 4-3-2-1 prospecting process acts as the production process for the model, ensuring a consistent and effective approach.

- **Strategy Enablement:** Sales plays enhance the prospecting process providing a step-by-step recipe for sellers to follow. Teaching, incentivizing, and resourcing your strategy properly transforms passive sellers into proactive prospectors, complementing the structured prospecting framework, turning outreach into engagements.

New Channel Math: This provides the system controls necessary to monitor and measure productivity, ensuring that the process is both effective and efficient.

Together, these innovations create a comprehensive framework that powers the effectiveness of partner engagements, driving measurable improvements in sales performance. In addition, MP3 tackles the common partnering challenges we encounter today. MP3 solves the issues associated with program-centric partner models addressing several critical areas:

One: Revenue Creation: MP3 transforms passive account managers into active sellers, revitalizing the sales process.

Two: Relevance: MP3 equips partner sellers with an easy-to-execute process, making it both feasible and profitable for partners to invest in proactive prospecting, thereby increasing the vendor's relevance within the partner ecosystem.

Three: Enablement: MP3 enhances retention by offering straightforward selling processes that simplify sales engagements and bridge the knowledge retention gap.

Four: Execution: The emphasis on structured coverage and targeted account mapping addresses the common execution challenges associated with passive sellers.

Five: ROI: By focusing on activating sellers, MP3 reduces channel costs by decreasing the need for recruiting new partners. The time-to-value improves as passive sellers become active. Additionally, the use of Ideal Customer Profiles (ICP) and relationship scoring enhances targeting accuracy, increasing engagement rates and opportunity flow.

MP3 brings ChannelOps to the forefront providing unprecedented visibility into strategy execution at both the seller and account levels. This new channel math addresses the partner attribution issue, enabling CROs to accurately attribute the value of the channel to the strategy execution within the partner ecosystem.

The MP3 Methodology is a flexible framework that seamlessly integrates with third-party technologies and services. MP3 incorporates digital selling technology and AI-driven prospecting tools. Additionally, MP3 supports Salesforce integration technologies for account mapping that enhance or substitute certain elements of the model. Our focus on flexibility and ease of integration ensures that the MP3 model remains adaptable and effective in leveraging the latest technological advancements to improve sales processes.

Finally, while various new engagement models and ecosystem partnering approaches are being introduced, only MP3 is a complete end-to-end solution sales acceleration model that can deliver profitable efficient growth, structured performance, true visibility and control. If you are seeking a more effective approach to partner-led revenue creation, It's time to join the MP3 Partner-Powered Revenue Revolution!

Figure 41.

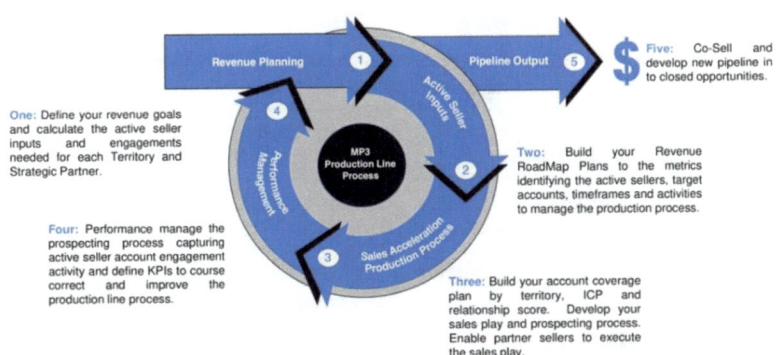

Call to Action!

As we reach the conclusion of this book, it's clear that the journey through structured performance models, strategic partner alignments, and innovative go-to-market strategies is just beginning. The insights and frameworks discussed are not purely academic; they are a call for action. I encourage you to take decisive steps toward transforming your organization's approach to partnerships and sales execution. Here's how you can start implementing change today:

One: Assess Your Model

Below is a simple assessment comparing your Partner Sale GTM Model with a Modern Structured Partner Performance Model. Is your Model Money? Let's find out.

Is Your Model Money?

The below survey will score your channel models readiness to optimize sales through your indirect sales channel.

	Assessment Questions	Yes	No
01	Are business plans and revenue targets collaboratively developed with strategic partners?		
02	Do your territory and partner revenue plans include sales metrics by solution, timeframes, target accounts, prospecting, and revenue activities?		
03	Are sales plays developed by solution to streamline selling efforts and enhance partner sales efficiency?		
04	Are partners trained to execute your solutions sales strategy using sales plays?		
05	Are accounts targeted and mapped with partners for prospecting as part of a structured territory plan?		
06	Are partner sellers provided enhanced incentives for prospecting and developing new sales?		
07	Do you incorporate a structured prospecting process like 4-3-2-1 to organize seller prospecting efforts?		
08	Is account engagement and prospecting activity tracked providing visibility and attribution to partner- target account outreach?		
09	Are partner sellers trained how to maximize revenue from each solution sale?		
10	Are new technologies such as digital selling and artificial intelligence integrated into your partner GTM process?		
11	Are Partner Account Managers measured on creating and scaling active sellers?		

- **Fat Stack:** If you answered "Yes" to 8 or more questions, congratulations! Your channel sales model is highly optimized, maximizing revenue through your partner community effectively. Your model is top-tier!

- **Small Stack:** If you answered "Yes" to 6-7 questions, well done! Your channel sales model is on a good path, incorporating many elements of a structured performance model. However, there are still opportunities for improvement to fully maximize your channel model's revenue-generating potential. Keep building those stacks!

- **Pocket Change:** If you answered "Yes" to 4-5 questions, you're making headway! Your channel model has started to adopt aspects of a structured performance partner sales model. However, significant improvements are necessary to truly maximize your channel model's potential for generating partner revenue. Consider this stage as pocket change, with much room to grow.

- **Your Broke:** If you answered "Yes" to fewer than 3 questions, your model needs substantial work. Your channel sales model currently lacks many critical aspects of a structured performance partner sales model, and significant enhancements are needed to boost your channel model's capacity to generate revenue. Here the model is costing considerably more than it is delivering and is destroying company value.

This assessment helps you identify the structured performance strengths and weaknesses of your current channel sales process. The assessment identifies areas of need to guide you in making targeted improvements to enhance your overall performance and revenue generation model.

Two: Embrace and Train

Adopt the ISAM and MP3 models within your organization. These frameworks are designed to streamline your go-to-market and partner management processes but will require buy-in across your organization. Invest in Channel Force training programs to educate your team on these new methodologies. Ensure that everyone, from sales to support staff, understands how these changes will benefit their roles and contribute to the organization's success.

Three: Execute and Iterate

Put your new strategies into action. Begin with pilot programs to manage risk and allow for adjustments before a full-scale rollout. I encourage companies to start with three partner account managers and territories to trial the process. This allows for data-driven insights from these initial implementations to refine your approach and validate the model. Remember, the goal is not only to implement a new system but to foster an environment of continual improvement and adaptation. Channel Force can help you integrate and implement the MP3 process into your current partner program and GTM model.

Four: Monitor, Measure, and Motivate

Regularly monitor the outcomes of your trial implementation and the performance of your partner sellers. Establish clear metrics for success and hold regular reviews to ensure you are on track. Celebrate the wins and analyze the losses for continuous learning. Keep your team motivated with clear goals and recognize their efforts in meeting new challenges.

Five: Leverage Technology

To truly maximize the performance of your structured performance model, consider utilizing the latest technologies. Tools for data analytics, partner relationship management, and customer engagement can provide the necessary infrastructure to execute MP3 more effectively. Invest in solutions that integrate well with your new processes and enhance your team's ability to perform. Channel Force offers a suite of tools to help deliver better performance including:

- **Planning IQ-** Planning IQ is the pioneering revenue planning tool tailored specifically for partnership models. This application leverages fourteen distinct data inputs to generate the necessary sales metrics for achieving set revenue goals. It provides a comprehensive revenue roadmap for each territory and partner, detailing the essential sales metrics needed by solution to meet your revenue objectives. Additionally, it outlines the timeframes for achieving these metrics, the resources required, and the financial investments necessary to support the efforts. Moving away from the outdated "Partner and Pray" models, Planning IQ emphasizes a "Plan and Perform" approach, enabling companies to model and predict revenue performance at both the territory and partner levels.

- **Performance IQ-** Is an innovative application that provides an intuitive and efficient way to capture and display vital data on partner and account-level prospecting activities, subsequently attributing the value of partner sellers during the sales development phase. Performance IQ ensures that performance metrics align seamlessly with the benchmarks set out in the Planning IQ revenue roadmap plan.

Performance IQ creates the ChannelOps Dashboards that paint a holistic picture of the channel's performance. Whether it's assessing the number of active sellers, gauging the breadth of accounts targeted, understanding customer engagement patterns and responses, or evaluating conversion rates and average deal sizes, Performance IQ covers it all. This attention to detail ensures that every aspect of the channel sales development process is accounted for, monitored, and optimized.

■ **Splashmentrics Digital Selling Solutions-** Splashmetrics introduces the first digital selling platform featuring an intelligent buyer's journey. This platform enables revenue leaders to tailor solution journeys by persona, guiding economic buyers through a process designed to educate, nurture, and compel them toward a purchase decision. These journeys offer dynamic content that adapts based on client interactions, ensuring a personalized experience. Crucially, all interactions are tracked, scored, and summarized in a comprehensive sales report. This cutting-edge technology is a game-changer, empowering partners to effectively generate new leads through their Account-Based Marketing (ABM) efforts. www.splashmetrics.com

■ **Ringdrop.ai-** Ringdrop.ai revolutionizes lead generation for marketing and sales teams through cutting-edge AI technology. By seamlessly integrating AI Virtual SDR (VSDR) capabilities, it eliminates the arduous tasks of prospect research, cold calling, and initial lead qualification.

Ringdrop.ai's AI Virtual SDR leverages Ideal Customer Profile data to pinpoint potential customers on LinkedIn. With user-provided insights on product value propositions and AI-generated probing questions, the VSDR initiates meaningful conversations via LinkedIn Connect requests. Once a prospect expresses interest, the VSDR seamlessly transfers lead profiles and conversation histories to sales personnel. www.ringdrop.ai

■ **Mindmatrix-** The foundational element of the MP3 technology stack is the partner portal, with Mindmatrix offering a next-generation solution that orchestrates engagements and communications essential for executing our structured performance process. Additionally, Mindmatrix enhances this foundation with advanced marketing automation, comprehensive partner management, and robust enablement capabilities that are integral to supporting the MP3 process. www.mindmatrix.net

■ **PartnerOptimizer-** PartnerOptimizer is a subscription-based SaaS platform designed for channel and partner ecosystem professionals which revolutionizes data intelligence for global B2B technology channel growth. Powered by our AI-engine, NeuralPartner™, the Partner Ecosystem Intelligence Platform provides instant, unparalleled insight into your Ideal Partner Profile (IPP) using thousands of business attributes to truly uncover the DNA of your best performers and find look a likes to force multiply revenues. www.partneroptimizer.com

Six: Advocate For Change

Be an advocate for change. Share your successes and learnings with your professional network. Your experiences can pave the way for broader industry shifts towards more efficient and effective partnership and sales strategies.

Figure 42.

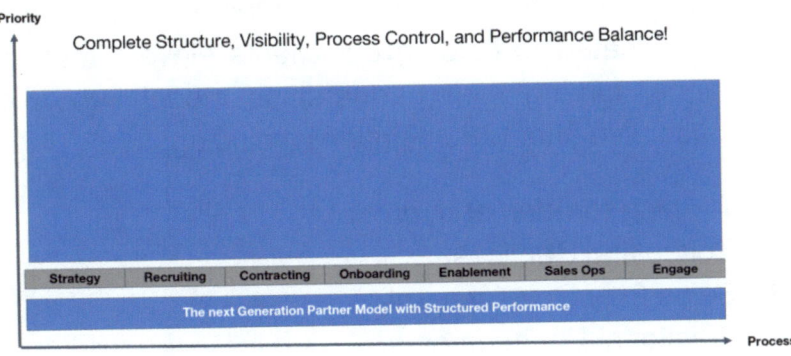

194

MP3 has laid the foundation to create a balanced approach to partnering where sales creation is prioritized and resourced equally with partner program centricity (See Figure 42), but the real work starts now. It's time to implement change. The future of our sales and partnership success depends on the actions we take today. Let's make it count.

Close

MP3 is not just a methodology; it's a call to action. Like the evolution from flip phones to smartphones, everything in the partnering landscape is advancing. Within the next five years, every modern partnering organization will be leveraging structured performance models equipped with ChannelOps tools. Partnerships will evolve to active sellers as the productivity measurement of the channel. Now is the time to embrace change. The future of the indirect sales model is here. Come join the partner-powered revenue revolution!

About Channel Force & Our Partners

If you're a CRO or Partner Pro looking to deliver profitable efficient revenue growth and want help delivering a structured performance model, lets connect! Channel Force specializes in Sales Acceleration Innovation, creating data-backed performance models. We have pioneered the "MP3 Sales Acceleration Methodology & ChannelOps Toolset." Channel Force is dedicated to helping our clients elevate their sales performance, turning their partnerships model into a profit powerhouse. We offer MP3 solutions including:

1. Training (on-demand, group)
2. Consulting Services
3. Sales Play Development
4. Fractional Engagements
5. Planning and Performance IQ Applications

Should you have any questions about the book or would like to explore our offerings feel free to schedule a meeting at www.channel-force.com or reachout to one of our partners.

Channel Force MP3 Partnerships

Procore Research Group- ProCore Resource Group is a proven and trusted consulting firm with expertise in Salesforce architecture, development techniques and business solutions for forward-thinking clients. We leverage Salesforce.com with our highly technical team and process re-engineering disciplines learned over many years of practice, resulting in over 600 successful implementations worldwide. Visit Procore Resources at www.procoreresources.com

Appizy- Appizy provides a solution for sharing and reusing technical calculations over the Internet. Appizy is a solution for converting spreadsheets into HTML/CSS/Javascript format in which the formulas remain active but are hidden from users. Only the input parameters are editable. Appizy also offers turnkey solutions for hosting calculation applications on the internet or intranet. www.appizy.com

Mindmatrix- Since its inception in 1998, Mindmatrix has been focused on helping companies sell more, faster. A pioneer of sales (direct & indirect) and marketing enablement technology, today Mindmatrix is the only company offering a fully unified platform (Bridge ™) that connects and enables sales (direct & indirect), marketing, alliances, and partner ecosystems. www.mindmatrix.net

Partner Trybe- At Partner Trybe we bring proven practices and methodologies from years of experience of having built partner ecosystem strategies from the ground up. Whether you are just getting started or would like to upgrade your current partner efforts, our Partner Chiefs are expert practitioners who can build and execute your ecosystem strategy for you. www.partnertrybe.com

Quantum Channels- Channelwise is a leading consulting services firm specializing in channel sales training offering a comprehensive suite of training modules that specifically address the unique needs of channel account managers, underscoring a singular commitment to nurturing superior channel management skills. www.quantum-channel.com

ACKNOWLEDGMENTS

After years of dedication to my first book, Channel Force, I had not planned on returning to writing another book. However, as I refined the structured performance strategies I advocate, I felt a strong pull to address some persistent challenges within the program-centric model. Writing a sequel has been far from a solo effort. I have been incredibly fortunate to work alongside many contributors whose insights and innovations have significantly enriched my thoughts and this book. I am grateful to several key individuals for their invaluable contributions and friendship. In no particular order:

- **Jay McBain, Chief Analyst and Influencer-** Jay is the worlds leading partnerships & ecosystems analyst. Jay was gracious enough to review the book and provide amazing insights and suggestions to improve the quality of the book. Thank you, Jay!

- **Cory Johnican, Channel Executive:** Cory played a crucial role in developing the Planning IQ framework and enhancing our approach to revenue planning.

- **Brent Earlewine, Channel Executive:** A pioneer of the MP3 process, Brent spent countless hours with me refining structured performance models, deeply influencing many of the ideas presented in this book.

- **Andre Becker, Founder Partner Trybe:** An exceptional thought leader, Andre has been instrumental in refining many of the book's concepts on structured performance and GTM best practices.

- **Rob Schade, CRO:** Rob's innovative thinking and meticulous editing skills have greatly shaped the narrative and content of this book. Rob is an innovation genius.

ACKNOWLEDGMENTS

- **Jake Zastrow, Channel Lead:** Jake not only helped develop the new ChannelOps equation during one of our consulting engagements but has also been a fervent advocate of the process in his own channel program.

- **Celio Rosa, Channel Executive:** Celio has been a critical sounding board and contributor, helping to shape the book's key concepts and contribution to the thought leadership of MP3.

- **Jen Waltz, Channel Executive:** An outstanding channel chief, Jen not only coined the book's title but also generously provided her editing expertise and valued opinions.

- **Brian Hattaway, Founder Procore:** The creator of the Performance IQ software, Brian has been a tremendous partner throughout the MP3 process.

- **Russ Schrader, Salesforce Developer:** Russ, a programming genius, crafted the code that powers the Performance IQ software.

- **Dan Libby, ChannelOps Genius:** A RevOps expert, Dan played a pivotal role in developing the formulas and concepts that underpin the Planning IQ Software. His contributions are fundamental.

- **Nicholas Hefti, Founder Appizy:** Nicholas dedicated considerable time to work with me on developing the Planning IQ application and has truly proven himself to be a star in the field. He is also the nicest person on the planet!

- **Mark Weingarten, Sales Executive:** A constant support at Channel Force, Mark has been involved in every facet of the project, offering his expertise and support throughout.

- **Kathryn Rose, Founder, ChannelWise:** Catherine has been a big supporter of Channel Force and is a great wealth of Marketing Knowledge.

- **Tom Walker, Channel Executive:** Tom is an amazing Channel and Distribution Leader who provided editing and thought leadership to improve the book.

- **Akash Singh, Partner Lead:** Akash was gracious enough to lend his editing services and suggestions to the book.

Each of these individuals has not only contributed their expertise but has also shared a vision of transforming traditional models to drive better outcomes. I am truly thankful for these amazing people and their friendships.

GLOSSARY OF TERMS

- **Active Seller** - An individual within a partner organization actively engaged in executing the 4-3-2-1 structured prospecting process.

- **Artificial Intelligence (AI)** - Technology that enables machines to mimic human intelligence, including decision-making and problem-solving capabilities.

- **Channel Sales Leadership** - The strategic management and leadership of indirect sales channels, typically involving partnerships and alliances to distribute products or services.

- **ChannelOps** - Operational aspects of managing and optimizing sales channels to improve efficiency and effectiveness in reaching end customers through partners.

- **Co-Sell** - A sales approach where a company collaborates with partners to sell products or services, sharing resources and leads to achieve mutual business goals.

- **CRM**- Customer relationship management (CRM) is a business strategy that uses data-driven software to manage, track, and store information about a company's customers.

- **Data-Driven Approach** - A methodology that emphasizes the use of data analytics and metrics to guide business decisions and strategies, ensuring outcomes are based on empirical evidence.

- **Data-Driven Revenue Planning** - A strategic approach that uses specific, quantifiable data to guide revenue generation activities and decisions, aiming to replace ambiguity with precision and actionable strategies.

■ **Ecosystem GTM Models** - Go-to-Market strategies that leverage a network of interconnected partners to deliver products or services to the market effectively.

■ **Edward Demming** - An influential American statistician, professor, author, lecturer, and consultant. Deming is best known for his work in the field of quality management, particularly the principles of continuous improvement and the use of statistical methods to reduce variability in manufacturing processes.

■ **ERP Systems**- A centralized system for businesses that enables every department to access and share common data to create a better work environment for every employee in the company.

■ **Frederick Taylor** - Often regarded as the father of scientific management, Taylor introduced methods to optimize human labor through time and motion studies, promoting the scientific training of workers and division of labor.

■ **Gantt Chart** - A visual tool for scheduling and monitoring project tasks, named after Henry Gantt, who expanded on earlier concepts to provide a comprehensive tool that became crucial in managing production and logistics during World War I.

■ **Harmonogram** - Developed by Karol Adamiecki, an early form of the Gantt chart that visually represented schedules in production processes, instrumental in planning and maintaining operations within a factory.

■ **Henry Gantt** - Known for developing the Gantt chart, he expanded on earlier scheduling concepts to create a tool for comprehensive task scheduling and monitoring in project management.

- **Ideal Customer Profile** - Is a detailed representation of a fictitious organization that best fits a company's products or services, encompassing characteristics such as industry, size, location, budget, pain points, and buying behaviors to effectively target and prioritize marketing and sales efforts.

- **Karol Adamiecki** - Developed the Harmonogram, an early precursor to the Gantt chart, which helped visualize schedules in production settings and contributed to the field of operational management.

- **Market Development Funds (MDF)** - Financial resources allocated to partners to support their marketing and sales activities, intended to drive demand and revenue generation for the vendor's solutions.

- **Martech-** MarTech describes the software marketers use to optimize their marketing efforts and achieve their objectives.

- **MP3 Methodology** - A structured approach to partner sales that integrates Methodology, Planning, Process, and Performance Management to transform partner sales into a systematic, predictable model.

- **Myers-Briggs Personality Test** - Also known as the Myers-Briggs Type Indicator (MBTI), is a widely used psychological assessment tool designed to measure individual personality traits.

- **Opportunistic Partnering Models** - Partnership approaches characterized by sporadic and unsystematic collaborations, typically lacking long-term strategy or structure.

- **Outreaches Needed** - The required number of engagements or interactions with potential economic buyers to meet sales targets, calculated based on the diversity of target personas and account coverage needs.

- **Partner and Pray** - An informal and unstructured approach to managing partnerships where success is largely left to chance rather than systematic efforts and processes.

- **Partner Ecosystem-** A complex network of interdependent relationships among multiple organizations, individuals, and resources, all working together to create value and drive innovation.

- **Partner Enablemen**t - The processes and tools provided to partners to empower them to effectively market, sell, and support a product or service.

- **Partner Impact Score:** A simple formula to measure the partner sales potential scoring: market reach, sales competency, sales priority, and discount structure.

- **Partner GTM Process** - The go-to-market strategies and activities undertaken by partners to market and sell products, which need to evolve to support proactive seller metrics and strategy execution.

- **Partner-Sourced Demand Creation** - Initiatives and strategies undertaken by partners to generate customer interest and demand for a product or service.

- **Partnership Leaders** - Executives or managers responsible for overseeing and driving the success of business partnerships within an organization.

- **Performance Management** - The practice of actively monitoring, evaluating, and directing the performance of individuals or groups within an organization to ensure that organizational goals are met efficiently and effectively.

- **Planning Metrics** - Key indicators used in the revenue planning process to measure and guide the achievement of sales targets through partner channels.

- **Profitable Efficient Growth (PEG)** - A business strategy focused on achieving growth not only through increased revenues but also by enhancing operational efficiency and maintaining profitability.

- **Resell** - The practice of purchasing a product or service and then selling it to another party, often with modifications or added value, as part of a business model.

- **Revenue Leaders** - Senior executives responsible for driving revenue growth and development within an organization, often including roles such as Chief Revenue Officer (CRO).

- **Revenue Operations (RevOps)** - An innovative approach to sales process management that integrates sales methodology and planning into a systematic, data-driven framework to optimize sales performance.

- **SAP System**- SAP is an acronym that stands for System Applications and Products in Data Processing. SAP collects, stores, and processes data across business applications and functions in one simplified platform.

- **Sales Acceleration** - Strategies and tools aimed at increasing the velocity of the sales process, improving sales performance, and reducing the time it takes to close deals.

- **Sales Creation Efforts** - Initiatives undertaken to generate sales opportunities, including lead generation, marketing campaigns, and customer outreach programs.

- **Scientific Management** - A management theory developed by Frederick Taylor that applies scientific methods to optimize labor productivity through the systematic training of workers and task specialization.

- **Solution Strength** - A simple formula that measures the sales potential for a solution to include assessing market need, solution fit and competitive strength.

- **Structured Account Mapping** - A methodical approach to defining which accounts will be targeted by partners, including detailed plans on how to engage and convert these accounts to achieve revenue goals.

- **Structured Performance** - A systematic approach to managing and evaluating performance with a focus on consistency, predictability, and adherence to predefined standards and objectives.

- **Territory Planning** - The process of setting and achieving sales objectives within a specific geographic or market segment, which involves detailed analysis and strategic alignment of partner capabilities and market opportunities.

- **Transparency** - The extent to which an organization openly communicates its activities, decisions, and operations, allowing stakeholders to have clear insight into its business practices.

Made in the USA
Columbia, SC
22 August 2024

40977413R00115